servant of Christ

ROGER ELLSWORTH

SERIES EDITOR: SIMON J ROBINSON

© Day One Publications 2012
First printed 2012

978-1-84625-295-2

Unless otherwise indicated, Scripture quotations are from the **New King James Version (NKJV)**®. Copyright © 1982 by Thomas Nelson, Inc. Used by permission. All rights reserved.

British Library Cataloguing in Publication Data available

Published by Day One Publications
Ryelands Road, Leominster, HR6 8NZ
Telephone 01568 613 740   FAX 01568 611 473

email—sales@dayone.co.uk
web site—www.dayone.co.uk

All rights reserved
No part of this publication may be reproduced, or stored in a retrieval system, or transmitted, in any form or by any means, mechanical, electronic, photocopying, recording or otherwise, without the prior permission of Day One Publications.

Cover design by Kathryn Chedgzoy
Printed by Orchard Press Cheltenham Ltd

In this excellent study of the life of Paul, Roger Ellsworth shows us that the apostle responded to the grace of God with a tireless passion for preaching the truth. As a man transformed by grace, Paul was compelled to take the message of the gospel wherever the Spirit led him, regardless of the inconvenience or danger. Pastor Ellsworth is gifted in connecting the events of the first century to challenges which face Christians today. Readers of this book will grow in their faith as they reflect on the amazing life and ministry of Paul. I highly recommend it.

Paul Hancock, M.D., Bible teacher and Vice President, Baptist St Anthony's Health System, Amarillo, TX, USA

A very helpful book about an incredible man. Roger Ellsworth achieves a work that is expository, theological and pastoral all in one.

Grant Gaines, Pastor, Calvary Baptist Church, Jackson, TN, USA

The following pages are dedicated to my son Tim,
who consistently models faithfulness
to the gospel of Christ.

Acknowledgements

I want to express many, many thanks to Simon Robinson and Jim Holmes for allowing me to participate in the Face2Face series. It is a good series, featuring the works of many fine authors. It is a blessing to be a part of it.

I also thank Suzanne Mitchell for her expert and invaluable guidance in the editing process.

I am also grateful to all who regularly attend Sunday evening worship services at Parkview Baptist Church. They heard in sermon form much of the material that is presented in the following pages. I am thankful for their faithfulness in hearing the preaching of the Word of God.

As always, I appreciate so very much the help of my wife, Sylvia, who willingly and capably assisted me in preparing these pages for publication.

Contents

● Chronology	8
● Introduction	10
❶ The trouble with twelve men (Acts 19:1–7)	12
❷ Those were the days! (Acts 19:8–20)	19
❸ A commotion in Ephesus (Acts 19:21–41)	25
❹ Insights from the tragedy of Eutychus (Acts 20:1–12)	31
❺ Paul and the Ephesian elders (Acts 20:13–38)	38
❻ Warned and ready (Acts 21:1–14)	48
❼ In Jerusalem (Acts 21:15–26)	55
❽ Suffering in Jerusalem (Acts 21:26–36)	60
❾ Addressing the mob (Acts 21:37–22:29)	68
❿ Standing for Jesus in a non-Jesus setting (Acts 22:30–23:11)	74
⓫ Cheering thoughts from chilling circumstances (Acts 23:11–35)	80
⓬ Voices from the cemetery (Acts 24:1–27)	86

⓭ Casual Festus (Acts 25:1–27) **92**

⓮ On trial for hope (Acts 26:1–15) **97**

⓯ Truths worth repeating (Acts 26:9–23) **102**

⓰ Dead men and modern positions (Acts 26:24–32) **108**

⓱ Good things in a bad storm (Acts 27:1–44) **114**

⓲ A wonderful shipwreck and a glorious snakebite (Acts 28:1–10) **121**

⓳ A chained man with an unchained message (Acts 28:11–31) **127**

Chronology

AD 30 The crucifixion, resurrection and ascension of Jesus

AD 32/33 Stephen is stoned (7:54–60); Saul is converted

AD 35/36 Paul's first visit to Jerusalem (9:26–28; Gal. 1:18–20)

AD 46 or 47 Paul's second visit to Jerusalem (11:27–30; Gal. 2:1–10)

AD 47/48 The first missionary journey (13–14)

AD 48 *Letter to the Galatians*

AD 49 The Council of Jerusalem (15:1–30)

The second missionary journey begins (15:36–18:22)

AD 50 *Letters to the Thessalonians*

AD 50–52 Paul in Corinth (18:1–18a)

AD 52 Paul returns to Syrian Antioch via Ephesus and Caesarea (18:18b–22)

The third missionary journey begins (18:23–21:17)

AD 52–55 Paul in Ephesus (19:1–20:1a)

AD 55–56 Paul in Macedonia (20:1b–2a)

Letters to the Corinthians

AD 56–57 Paul winters in Corinth (20:2b–3a)

early AD 57 *Letter to the Romans*

AD 57 The voyage to Jerusalem via Macedonia, Troas and Miletus (20:3b–21:17)

Paul is arrested in Jerusalem (21:27–36) and tried before Felix (24:1–22)

AD 57–59 Paul's Caesarean imprisonment (23:23–24:27)

AD 59 Paul is tried before Festus and Agrippa (25:6–26:32)

AD 59–60 The voyage to Rome (27:1–28:16)

AD 60–62 Paul's Roman imprisonment (28:16–31)

The Prison Epistles written (Ephesians, Philippians, Colossians, Philemon)

The Pastoral Epistles written (1, 2 Timothy, Titus)

AD 64 or 65 Possible trip to Spain/The martyrdom of Paul in Rome[1]

Note

1 Adapted from the chronological tables of Colin Hemer; cited by **John R. W. Stott** in *The Spirit, the Church and the World* (Leicester: InterVarsity Press, 1990), pp.18–19; and **F. F. Bruce,** *Paul: Apostle of the Heart Set Free* (Grand Rapids, MI: Eerdmans, 1977), p. 475.

Introduction

There have been times when the church of Christ has been remarkably clear-headed, times when she has understood the reality of human sin and the certainty of divine judgement. There have been times when the church has believed deeply in the power of the gospel of Jesus Christ to save people from their sins and to give them a right standing with the holy God before whom they must finally stand.

Now is not one of those times. Thank God, however, that the gospel is not entirely silent these days. It is still being faithfully sounded out here and there. But much of the church and her leadership are firmly in the grip of a 'growth-mania': numerical growth at any cost! If we are to grow our churches, we must give people what they like and not give them what they don't like! So there is little talk today about sin, judgement and the saving work of the Lord Jesus Christ. One could go to many church services and never get the slightest impression that the doctrinal core of Christianity is ruin by sin, redemption by Christ and regeneration by the Holy Spirit.

All sorts of bizarre things are going on under the banner of Christianity these days! Wrestling, parachuting, seeking to set the world record for the amount of time required to duct-tape someone to a wall! What's next?

It's time to name the diseases that are afflicting so much of the church today: apathy, nominalism, heresy and apostasy!

The modern church needs a spiritual tonic to flush the

toxins from her system and to bring her back to health. We find such a tonic in Luke's account of the ministry of the apostle Paul. What a man was this Paul! Plucked from the guilt of his sin by the sovereign God, he went throughout the Mediterranean world to share boldly the glorious gospel of Jesus Christ.

As we trace Paul's ministry through the second half of Acts (chs. 19–28), we must surely marvel at the apostle's faithfulness to the gospel. No matter where we find him—in Ephesus, in Jerusalem, in courts of law, on board a ship, on a remote island, or under house arrest in Rome—we find unswerving allegiance to the gospel.

As we retrace the great apostle's proclamation of the gospel, let us pray that God will rekindle in our hearts his passion for the gospel.

1 The trouble with twelve men

(Acts 19:1–7)

In these verses we find the apostle Paul returning to the city of Ephesus, having made only a brief stop there some months earlier (18:18–21). When he arrived in the city he met twelve men whom Luke identifies as 'disciples' (v. 1). Furthermore, Luke's account suggests that these men either had been introduced to Paul or had introduced themselves to him as baptized believers (vv. 2–3). But something about these men did not 'ring true' with the apostle. Man of discernment that he was, Paul detected a flaw or lack in these men. There were all kinds of disciples and believers in Paul's day, even as there are today. So he was not quick to conclude that these men were truly believers in or disciples of Jesus.

EXAMINATION OF BELIEF (VV. 2–3)

The first task before Paul was to zero in on the true spiritual condition of these men. So he asked a 'diagnostic' question. In other words, he posed a question that would enable him to determine their spiritual condition. His question was whether they had received the Holy Spirit when they believed (v. 2).

Paul knew how the Spirit was operating in those days. Every time the gospel broke through a major barrier and went to a new group of people, that breakthrough was accompanied by special signs from the Holy Spirit. This was necessary to demonstrate publicly and visibly that these groups had been incorporated into one body, namely, the body of Christ. This had happened when the gospel went to Samaria (8:14-17) and to the Gentiles (10:44-48).

But nothing of this sort had happened with these men. So they responded to Paul's question in this way: 'We have not so much as heard whether there is a Holy Spirit' (v. 2).

This led Paul to ask another question: 'Into what then were you baptized?' (v. 3). And their answer was, 'Into John's baptism' (v. 3).

So Paul was able to make his diagnosis. These men were not Christians at all. They were, in the words of Dennis E. Johnson, 'a residual pocket of Old Testament anticipatory faith that had somehow been bypassed by the news of Jesus' redemptive work'.[1]

The men in this passage had a kind of faith, but it was not real faith. It was a faith in John the Baptist and the baptism he practised rather than faith in the Lord Jesus Christ, to whom John the Baptist pointed. But prior to their visit from Paul, these men had probably assumed that they were OK.

The sobering message of these verses is that it is possible to be a type of religious believer without being truly saved. Sadly enough, this is a message that is much needed. There is reason to believe that many church members are in this very position. They have a kind of religion, but they are not truly saved. It could very well be that the greatest opportunities most churches have for evangelism are among a large percentage of their members!

PRESENTATION OF THE LORD JESUS (VV. 4–5)

There was certainly nothing wrong with John the Baptist's baptism when he was practising it. John was sent by God, and the baptism he practised was approved by God. But John and his ministry were designed to point to the Lord Jesus Christ. After Jesus came John gave way to him, and his baptism was intended to give way to Christian baptism, which pictures the redeeming work of Christ.

Luke quite deliberately connects these twelve men with Apollos, the Alexandria-born Jew who was 'eloquent' and 'mighty in the Scriptures' (18:24). Like the twelve men in Ephesus, Apollos also 'knew only the baptism of John' (18:25). But Luke plainly declares that Apollos also knew the truth about the Lord Jesus (18:28), and, while in Ephesus and with instruction from Aquila and Priscilla (18:26), came to understand Christian baptism. So Luke uses Apollos as something of a reference point to help us see the true spiritual condition of the twelve men of Ephesus, who differed from Apollos in this respect: while Apollos 'knew only the baptism of John', he also knew 'the way of the Lord' (18:25); that is, he knew the full truth about Jesus. The twelve men at Ephesus evidently did not know about Jesus at all. Albert Barnes offers this assessment of them: 'It does not even appear that they had heard that the Messiah had come, or had heard of Jesus of Nazareth.'[2]

So the trouble with these twelve men was that they had never come to faith in Christ! We should not be surprised, then, to read these words: 'Then Paul said, "John indeed baptized with a baptism of repentance, saying to the people that they should believe on Him who would come after him, that is, on Christ Jesus"' (v. 4). Paul's message to these men was to believe in Jesus in order to be saved from their sins. That is still God's message to all of us. The best statement of it is in these well-known words: 'For God so loved the world that He gave His only begotten Son, that whoever believes in Him should not perish but have everlasting life' (John 3:16).

So if you want to be saved, you must believe in Jesus. This is not a matter of simply agreeing with the facts about Jesus. It is rather committing your hope for forgiveness of your sins and a right standing with God to what Jesus has done on the cross. And if you have believed in Jesus, you should rejoice with joy unspeakable and full of glory.

Many take this passage the wrong way. They assume that these twelve men had accepted the Lord Jesus Christ as their Saviour and now only needed to be baptized by the Holy Spirit. In other words, they suggest that the Christian experience consists of two tiers. The first tier is receiving Christ as Saviour, and the second is receiving the Holy Spirit.

Those who hold this position maintain that one can have the first tier and not the second. That, they say, was the case with these twelve men.

But if that had been the case, the apostle Paul would have said something along these lines: 'You have been saved, but you now need to take the next step. And I am going to tell you how to be baptized by the Holy Spirit.'

But that is not what Paul said. Instead, he pointed these men to the Lord Jesus Christ. Frederick Dale Bruner writes of Paul, 'on learning of their ignorance of the Holy Spirit Paul's subject, surprisingly, was not the Holy Spirit, it was Jesus Christ.'[3]

Those who teach the two-tier experience for Christians

sometimes make it seem as if receiving the Holy Spirit is a far greater matter than receiving the Lord Jesus. But that is all wrong! The Holy Spirit himself came to glorify the Lord Jesus (John 15:26; 16:14), and he is grieved when we place him above the Lord Jesus and pleased when we honour the Lord Jesus.

After hearing the message of Christ from the apostle Paul, these twelve men were 'baptized in the name of Jesus' (v. 5).

CULMINATION (V. 6)

After these men were baptized, Luke adds these words: 'And when Paul had laid hands on them, the Holy Spirit came upon them, and they spoke with tongues and prophesied.'

What we have here is a miniature reproduction of what occurred on the Day of Pentecost (2:1–13). The gift of tongues, far from being unintelligible gibberish, was the ability to speak in languages never learned. The gift of prophecy amounted to receiving direct revelation from God and transmitting it to others.

Those who are eager to make these and other extraordinary gifts the norm for believers in every age ignore the special nature of what occurred on Pentecost, at Caesarea (10:44–48) and at Ephesus. In each case, the gospel was making inroads into a significant area, and it was essential, in the words of John R. W. Stott, 'to demonstrate visibly and publicly that particular groups were incorporated into Christ by the Spirit'.[4] Frederick Dale Bruner offers this helpful summary regarding Pentecost, Caesarea and Ephesus: 'Speaking in tongues in Acts is on all three occasions a corporate, church-founding, group-conversion phenomenon, and never the subsequent Spirit-experience of an individual.'[5]

It is lamentable that a passage that was so clearly designed by the Holy Spirit to cast the spotlight on the importance of receiving the Lord Jesus (vv. 4–5) is so often construed in such a way that the spotlight is diverted from Christ. Let us always seek to remember that the Holy Spirit came to glorify the Lord Jesus. We can rest assured that he is always pleased when we focus on Jesus and displeased when we focus more on him than on Jesus.

FOR FURTHER STUDY

1. Read Romans 8:9. What does Paul teach in this verse? What are the implications of this verse for those who believe in two-tier salvation?
2. Read 1 Corinthians 12:13. What does Paul teach in this verse?
3. Read John 15:26 and 16:13. What does Jesus affirm in these verses about the nature of the work of the Holy Spirit?

TO THINK ABOUT AND DISCUSS

1. What questions should we ask people today to determine their spiritual condition? Do you think that we can form an accurate assessment merely from hearing their answers to our questions, or are there other aspects we must take into account?
2. How would you respond to those who suggest that receiving the Holy Spirit is something that happens after conversion and which is greater than conversion?
3. In what ways do some churches place too much emphasis on the Holy Spirit? Do you think that other churches react to this by placing too little emphasis on his work? If so, how?

Notes

1 **Dennis E. Johnson,** *Let's Study Acts* (Edinburgh: Banner of Truth, 2003), p. 235.
2 **Albert Barnes,** *Barnes' Notes: Acts, Romans* (Grand Rapids, MI: Baker, 2005), p. 275.
3 **Frederick Dale Bruner,** *A Theology of the Holy Spirit* (Grand Rapids, MI: Eerdmans, 1970), p. 209.
4 **John R. W. Stott,** *The Spirit, the Church and the World* (Downers Grove, IL: InterVarsity Press, 1990), p. 305.
5 **Bruner,** *A Theology of the Holy Spirit*, p. 192.

2 Those were the days!

(Acts 19:8–20)

When we are looking back with fondness on bygone days, we may exclaim, 'Those were the days!' Perhaps we find ourselves looking back to those days when we fell in love or when our children were little. We could even find ourselves looking back to wonderful days of blessing in our churches.

Imagine with me now an old Christian couple living in Ephesus years after the apostle Paul completed his ministry there. Let's call them Clyde and Carol Christian. Both Clyde and Carol had come to faith in the Lord Jesus as Paul preached in Ephesus. Both had witnessed the many evidences of the mighty moving of the Spirit of God in their town. Now, on the day we are imagining, Clyde and Carol are sitting in their rocking chairs and recalling it all, and Clyde remarks, 'Those were the days!'

As those words fall from his lips, his two grandchildren come through the door. Hearing their grandfather's exclamation, they immediately ask, 'Which days are you talking about, Grandpa?' And, of course, he says, 'Your grandmother and I were just talking about those wonderful days when the apostle Paul was preaching here in Ephesus.'

That response prompts yet another question from those inquisitive grandchildren: 'Grandpa, what made those such wonderful days?' I would not be at all surprised if the old grandfather says something along these lines: 'They were wonderful days because they were both ordinary and extraordinary.'

ORDINARY DAYS (VV. 8–10)
We often sigh over the ordinariness of our days. Following the same routine wearies us. We want something new and different and exciting. When we are in the midst of ordinary days, we seriously doubt that we will ever look back and say, 'Those were the days!'

But the very ordinariness that makes us sigh can be a tremendous blessing if we would only allow ourselves to ponder deeply.

Paul preached for two years in Ephesus. This was the closest he ever came to a settled ministry. People went to hear him preach again and again. It became an ordinary thing—but, oh, the blessedness of that ordinary thing! Hearing the great apostle unfold the riches of God's saving grace! That ordinary thing was extraordinary! I can well imagine those blessed hearers saying years later, 'Those were the days!'

It's interesting how we prize ordinariness in other areas of life. If we tune into the Food Channel, we might very well hear a chef boast, 'We have never changed the recipe for this dish.' And everyone approves and talks about how wonderful it is that no changes have been made.

But people employ a different standard in regard to the church. A pastor says that he is preaching the same message as he was many years ago and his church is offering the same ministry, and people get upset. We must change to keep up with the times! We must try the new and the novel! We must be more entertaining and funnier! We must not expect people to embrace an old message and an old ministry!

May God help us to prize the kind of ministry that Paul performed in Ephesus: the constant exposition of the Word of God! If we do not appreciate the ordinary ministry of the Word of God, we can be sure that it is because we do not appreciate the extraordinary nature of the Word of God.

But Clyde and Carol Christian could also look back with fondness on Paul's days in Ephesus because they were also …

EXTRAORDINARY DAYS (VV. 11–20)

We might say that the ordinary preaching of God's Word led to extraordinary results.

EXTRAORDINARY POWER (VV. 11–12)

One of the extraordinary things during Paul's ministry in Ephesus was the miracles that occurred. Luke calls attention to them by terming them 'unusual miracles' (v. 11), or, we might say, 'miracle miracles'!

We should note that it was God, not Paul, who did the miracles (v. 11). Mere men do not work miracles!

This was not the only time that miracles took place in connection with the ministry of Paul (see 14:3), but there seems to have been an explosion of miracles in his ministry at Ephesus. Why was this the case? Warren Wiersbe observes, 'God enabled Paul to perform "special miracles" because Ephesus was a center for the occult … and Paul was demonstrating God's power right in Satan's territory.'[1]

These miracles were of such an unusual nature that 'even

handkerchiefs or aprons were brought from his [Paul's] body to the sick, and the diseases left them and the evil spirits went out of them' (v. 12).

This is the only instance in Scripture of miracles of healing occurring in this way. What was the purpose behind these miracles? God was endorsing his apostle so that the people in Ephesus would heed his preaching. God works in different ways at different times. We err if we try to make extraordinary days into ordinary days; that is, if we think that God must work in the same way at all times.

EXTRAORDINARY FEAR (VV. 13-17)

The miracles that God worked through Paul in Ephesus worked in a way that Paul would probably never have imagined. Seeing Paul cast out evil spirits caused 'some of the itinerant Jewish exorcists' to attempt to do the same (v. 13).

They soon learned that the name of Jesus was not a mere magical potion that people could use at any time to get what they wanted! The evil spirit they attempted to exorcise responded by saying, 'Jesus I know, and Paul I know; but who are you?' (v. 15). The man whom that spirit was possessing 'leaped on them, overpowered them, and prevailed against them, so that they fled out of that house naked and wounded' (v. 16).

So the unusual miracles of Paul led to unusual fear, and 'the name of the Lord Jesus was magnified' (v. 17).

People in Ephesus, both Jews and Greeks (v. 17), learned that the name of Jesus is a holy name—not like any other name—and it must be treated with reverence. What will it take to convince us of the same?

EXTRAORDINARY REPENTANCE (VV. 18–20)

The great power of Paul's ministry in Ephesus and the great fear it created teamed up to cause a genuine and widespread repentance.

Many believed in the Lord Jesus, and the genuineness of their faith was indicated by their 'confessing and telling their deeds' (v. 18). There were also many who abandoned their practice of magic by bringing their books and burning them 'in the sight of all' (v. 19). The value of all these books came to 50,000 pieces of silver (v. 19)! What a bonfire! What repentance!

Many these days contend that it is possible to be truly saved by the Lord Jesus Christ from their sins while they go right on practising those very same sins! But this is a lie from the devil himself. True faith in Christ changes us, and if we are not changed, we are not saved.

The ministry of Paul in Ephesus was, then, a Word-centred, Christ-exalting, life-changing ministry. How we need such ministries today! Let us be praying for such. Let us pound heaven with our prayers until the same can be said of these days as Luke wrote of those days: 'So the word of the Lord grew mightily and prevailed' (v. 20).

FOR FURTHER STUDY

1. Do a study on the miracles reported in the Bible. Would you say that they are evenly distributed throughout, or that they are concentrated in certain eras? Why do you think this is the case?
2. Read Luke 19:8. How did Zacchaeus manifest true repentance? What other examples can you find in the Bible of people who changed their lives as a result of turning to God?

TO THINK ABOUT AND DISCUSS

1. Try to think of an era in your church's life that might have caused the members to exclaim, 'Those were the days!' What made those days special?
2. How would you respond to a fellow-church member who complains about the pastor's ordinary ministry of preaching the Word of God? Why do you think that people complain in this way?

Note

1 **Warren W. Wiersbe,** *The Bible Exposition Commentary*, vol. i (Wheaton, IL: Victor Books, 1989), p. 481.

3 A commotion in Ephesus

(Acts 19:21–41)

Paul was making plans to go to other places (vv. 21–22) when trouble arose in Ephesus. Matthew Henry takes note of Paul's planning and says of him, 'He was a man of vast designs for God, and was for making his influences as widely diffusive as might be.'[1] Let's learn from this that we too should have 'vast designs' for God.

The trouble in Ephesus, termed by Luke 'a great commotion' (v. 23), was caused by a man named Demetrius. Let's learn from this that one person can hinder the work of God.

Demetrius was a manufacturer of miniature 'silver shrines of Diana' (v. 24). Albert Barnes identifies Diana as 'one of the twelve superior deities' who was worshipped under several names in several countries, but 'the most celebrated place of her worship was Ephesus, a city peculiarly dedicated to her'.[2]

Demetrius supplied the miniature silver shrines he made to local merchants, who sold them to the people. The whole venture was very profitable.

When Demetrius saw the success of Paul's ministry, he also saw his profits going up in smoke. So he called a meeting of his fellow-tradesmen and got them enflamed and enraged against Paul (vv. 25–28). These men, in turn, managed to get the people of the city stirred up.

THE CONTEXT OF THE COMMOTION (VV. 21–23)

Paul was in the midst of closing out his ministry in Ephesus. It had been a good and productive ministry. He was making plans for the future. Luke makes it clear that all this was in accordance with the leadership of the Holy Spirit (v. 21). It was, then, in the context of usefulness, spiritual power and closeness to God that the commotion arose (v. 23). Some would have us believe that if we live close enough to God, no problems or difficulties will come our way. This is a delusion. We never advance so far in spirituality that we are beyond the reach of trouble (vv. 21, 23).

THE CAUSE OF THE COMMOTION (VV. 24–27)

What caused the commotion? Was it because Paul had organized a protest against the temple of Diana? Had he and other believers picketed the temple? Had they circulated a petition to close it? Had they staged anti-idolatry rallies? What was all the fuss about?

Warren Wiersbe answers by saying of Paul, 'All he did was teach the truth daily and send out his converts to witness to the lost people in the city. As more and more people got converted, fewer and fewer customers were available.'[3] With the word 'customers' Wiersbe is referring, of course, to those who, had they not been converted, would have been purchasing the silver temples from Demetrius.

So it was Paul's preaching that changed the dynamics in Ephesus. What was it that Paul was preaching? It was the same message that he preached everywhere—the message of Jesus Christ. More particularly, Paul was declaring that by virtue of his resurrection from the dead, Jesus had decisively demonstrated that he alone is Lord and Saviour. This meant that Diana was not God or Lord or Saviour (v. 26).

We will not encounter much opposition if we are content to preach an ambiguous message, but let us plainly declare the truth about Jesus and we will find out what opposition is.

Why are people so opposed to this message? It offends their self-esteem because it tells them they are sinners and can do nothing to help themselves. It offends their love for tolerance and pluralism in that it says there is only one way of salvation. It offends their intellectual sophistication in that it says salvation is through a Jewish carpenter shedding his blood on a Roman cross two thousand years ago!

THE CONFUSION IN THE COMMOTION (VV. 28–34)

Luke's description of the riot in Ephesus makes it clear that most of the people sided with Demetrius.

This is a classic example of mob action. Benjamin Franklin said that a mob is 'a monster with heads enough, but no brains'.[4] Max Lerner wrote, 'Every mob ... is a League of Frightened Men that seeks reassurance in collective action.'[5] Luke also declares that most of the people did not know what was going on (vv. 29, 32).

Many people today are confused about what is true and what is not. They are merely carried along by the tide of popular opinion, parroting what others are saying. The fact that people have numbers and strong feelings on their side does not mean that they are right.

THE CONSOLATION FROM THE COMMOTION (VV. 35–41)

After considerable confusion among the rioting mob, the city

clerk was finally able to take the situation in hand. He did so by pointing out the following:
- Paul and his companions had neither committed sacrilege (robbing the temple) nor blasphemy (speaking evil of the goddess Diana) (v. 37).
- Demetrius and his fellow-craftsmen had legal avenues available to them if they had a legitimate case (vv. 38–39).
- By creating an 'uproar', the citizens of Ephesus were inviting scrutiny and perhaps punishment from the Roman government.

The reasoning of the clerk won the day, and the crowd dispersed (v. 41).

It is the clerk's opening statement that screams for attention. He claimed that everyone agreed that the city of Ephesus had been entrusted with the keeping of the temple of Diana and of 'the image which fell down from Zeus' (v. 35). The image to which this man referred was a wooden image of Diana that was so old that it predated their temple, which had been renovated seven times! This image was so old that its maker had been forgotten. So the people of Ephesus explained its existence by saying that Zeus had sent it down from heaven!

So as far as this man was concerned, the religion of Diana was so old and well established that its adherents did not need to fear this new religion that Paul was advancing. He was rebuking his fellow-citizens for allowing themselves to be caught up by a groundless fear.

Was he right? Let Warren Wiersbe answer:

Ephesus is gone, and so is the worldwide worship of Diana of the Ephesians. The city and the temple are gone, and the silversmiths' guild is gone. Ephesus is a place visited primarily by archeologists and people on Holy Land tours. Yet the Gospel of God's grace and the church of Jesus Christ are still here! We have four inspired letters that were sent to the saints in Ephesus—Ephesians, 1 and 2 Timothy, and Revelation 2:1–7. The name of Paul is honored, but the name of Demetrius is forgotten.[6]

The religion of Diana failed and Christianity prevailed because the former was merely the figment of people's imaginations while the latter was indeed the product of the true God sending something (or rather, Someone) down from heaven—the Lord Jesus Christ. Because God sent him and because he, the Lord Jesus, is God, Christianity can perish only if God himself perishes.

Christianity will continue to be attacked as long as the world lasts, but 'the gates of Hades' cannot prevail against it (Matt. 16:18).

FOR FURTHER STUDY

1. Read 2 Timothy 3:12. What does Paul promise Timothy in this verse? Why is this the case? Read Psalm 34:19. What comfort does David promise in this verse?
2. Read Philippians 2:9–11. What does Paul affirm in these verses regarding Jesus? What does this mean for other gods and for those who serve them?

TO THINK ABOUT AND DISCUSS

1. What opposition do you see towards Christianity today? How do you explain such opposition? What do you consider to be the proper response to this opposition?

2. Can you think of times—whether in your own life, in the life of someone you know or in the life of your church—when a period of great spiritual usefulness has been interrupted by trouble of some kind? Why do you think this happens? Should Christians feel defeated when this happens? Explain your answer.

3. Can you think of other false religions or philosophies, like the worship of Diana, that were once very popular but are now extinct? Now identify some of the false religions of our day. Should Christians fear or not fear these religions, and why or why not?

Notes

1 **Matthew Henry,** *Matthew Henry's Commentary*, vol. vi (Tappan, NJ: Fleming H. Revell, [no date]), p. 251.
2 **Albert Barnes,** *Barnes' Notes: Acts, Romans* (Grand Rapids, MI: Baker, 2005), p. 281.
3 **Warren W. Wiersbe,** *The Bible Exposition Commentary*, vol. i (Wheaton, IL: Victor Books, 1989), p. 482.
4 Quoted in Ibid.
5 Quoted in Ibid.
6 Ibid., p. 483.

4 Insights from the tragedy of Eutychus

(Acts 20:1–12)

In the first six verses of Acts 20, Luke provides 'place', 'time' and 'people' details. With the 'place' details, Luke traces Paul's departure from Ephesus, the scene of the commotion described in the previous chapter, to Macedonia (v. 1), Greece (v. 2) and Macedonia again (v. 3). With the 'time' details, Luke lets us know that the first stop in Macedonia was merely a matter of passing through (v. 2), while the stay in Greece lasted for three months (v. 3).

With his 'people' details, Luke identifies those who accompanied Paul at this time: Sopater, Aristarchus, Secundus, Gaius, Timothy, Tychicus and Trophimus. One cannot read these names without being reminded of Paul's ability to influence men profoundly for the glory of Christ. This quality is something that we should all seek to emulate, knowing as we do that we will never be able to match the great apostle. But we can all do something in this area.

Place, time and people were variables in Paul's ministry. But there were invariables as well. One was the content of his Christ-centred ministry. We can rest assured that the 'encouraged' of verse 2 refers to encouraging his hearers with the truths of the Lord. Another invariable was opposition, which at this point took the form of a plot against Paul that forced him to return to Macedonia for a seven-day stay in the city of Troas. While engaged in ministry there, Paul was involved in the fascinating event described by Luke in verses 7–12.

This passage gives us information about the worship of the early Christians. It was held on the first day of the week. It included the Lord's Supper and it included preaching. But Luke did not write this passage to tell us about the nature of worship in those days. He wrote rather to tell us about a young man named Eutychus. While Paul preached in an upper room, Eutychus was overcome with sleep and fell to the street below. When the others reached him, he was dead.

This is a much-abused passage. It is frequently used by preachers to poke fun at those who fall asleep during sermons, and it is often used by church members to poke fun at preachers for preaching long sermons.

But if you and I had been there that night, we would not have been laughing. I can assure you that Eutychus's parents were not laughing. Neither were his friends. And the apostle Paul was not laughing. This was a tragedy of immense proportions.

Why did Luke see fit to include this account? He did not do so to warn us about sleeping in church or about preaching long sermons. He rather did so to draw our attention to some issues that are just as vital and important today as they were on that long-ago occasion.

The first of these issues is ...

THE FRAGILE NATURE OF LIFE IN THIS WORLD

We often forget this. We get accustomed to the steady, rhythmic succession of days. We make our plans and carry them out while hitting only a bump or two.

Before we realize it, we have been lulled into a sleep of our own. It begins to seem to us that life is stretching out endlessly before us. We know about death, but it seems far away. It certainly won't come to us, at least not until we are very old! We can even get to the point that we regard ourselves as being entitled to long lives. Anything less would be unfair!

While we know theoretically that life is uncertain and death is sure, we can easily begin to live as if the reverse were true!

Eutychus rises from the pages of Scripture to remind us that death is constantly on the prowl and can at any moment pounce on us. Eutychus was young, but he died. Eutychus probably thought he was perfectly safe. What could be safer than going to church? But he died.

We are wise if we live with the awareness of death. We are wise if we frequently remind ourselves of how very thin is the line between this life and eternity. We are wise if we take as our own the words of David: 'there is but a step between me and death' (1 Sam. 20:3). And we are wise if we prepare to face death.

A second issue presented to us by the tragedy of Eutychus is …

THE PERPLEXING NATURE OF THE WAYS OF GOD
Would you agree that Eutychus was the victim of certain natural laws? He slept because he was tired. He fell because he slept. He died because he fell.

Would you also agree that God put these laws in place and that he can, when he so desires, suspend these laws?

Would you further agree that God loves his children?

If we are in agreement on each of these matters, we have in

the case of Eutychus a cause for great perplexity. Why did God allow Eutychus to die? Why did he not step in and suspend the laws of nature to protect Eutychus? Why did he wait until after Eutychus died to step in? Why did he allow the family and friends of Eutychus to go through these moments of agony?

This situation reminds us of the death of Lazarus in John 11. You remember that Lazarus's sisters, Mary and Martha, sent word to Jesus that Lazarus was sick while there was still time for Jesus to come and heal him.

But Jesus let Lazarus die! Only then did he come to Mary and Martha! Why did Jesus delay? Why did he allow Lazarus to die and Mary and Martha to go through heart-wrenching grief and sorrow? Jesus himself gave the answer: 'This sickness is not unto death, but for the glory of God, that the Son of God may be glorified through it' (John 11:4).

Here is a theological principle to guide us when our circumstances become so utterly bewildering that we wonder what God is doing: God always has bigger fish to fry than meets the eye!

I am asking you to do something that is very difficult indeed. I am asking you to believe that God is always at work in the midst of our circumstances for our good and for his glory (Rom. 8:28).

What did God accomplish through the fall and the death of Eutychus? In addition to what we have already noticed—namely, reminding people of the fragile nature of this life—the Lord used this instance to authenticate Paul as his apostle so that people would be more inclined to believe his message about the Lord Jesus Christ. We might say that the death of Eutychus furthered the gospel of Christ!

That brings us to consider a third matter presented to us by the tragedy of Eutychus:

THE HOPEFUL NATURE OF OUR FAITH
I have said that God used the death of Eutychus to validate Paul as his apostle so that people would believe his message. Here is part of the message of Paul: the bodies of all believers will be raised from the dead just as surely as Eutychus was raised.

We find Paul's teaching on this in 1 Thessalonians 4:13–18. In this passage he declares that the Lord Jesus himself will return from heaven with a shout, with the voice of the archangel and with a blast from the trumpet of God. Then the bodies of those who have died in faith in the Lord Jesus Christ will spring from their graves and those bodies will be rejoined to their souls, which went to be with the Lord at the moment of death.

But the resurrection of dead believers will be different from Eutychus's resurrection. He was raised to resume this life and to die again. When Jesus comes again, believers will be raised to eternal glory, where there will be no crying, no pain, no sorrow and no more death!

This message is of such a nature that we would never dare to believe it, were it not for the fact that God has provided authentication of his Word! We can believe this message! It comes to us from God's apostle!

Luke records the response of the people to the restoration of Eutychus to life: 'they were not a little comforted' (v. 12). And Paul, God's apostle, wraps up his teaching on the resurrection of all believers with these words: 'Therefore comfort one another with these words' (1 Thes. 4:18).

What comfort there is in knowing that God's people will be raised to eternal glory! But that comfort applies only to God's people; that is, it applies only to those who have faith in the Lord Jesus Christ. So the most important business in this life is to make sure that we have received him. If we have, we should rejoice. If we have not, we should not delay.

FOR FURTHER STUDY

1. Read James 4:13–16. What does James teach here about the nature of life in this world?
2. Read Romans 11:33–36. What does Paul assert about the ways of God? What should our response be?
3. Read 1 Peter 1:3. How does Peter describe the Christian's hope? What is the basis of it?

TO THINK ABOUT AND DISCUSS

1. In what ways does the world try to deal with the unpredictability of life and the certainty of death? Think, for example, about the euphemisms used to refer to death, the use of humour, and taboos related to death. How can Christians help people to face up to the subject seriously?
2. Discuss whether it is wise—even healthy—for Christians to think frequently about the unpredictability of this life and the certainty of death.
3. 'God always has bigger fish to fry than meets the eye.' Does this statement encourage you in a particular circumstance you are currently facing?
4. How would you respond to someone who asks why God lets people suffer?

5. How would you comfort someone who is mourning the death of a believer? Which Scripture verses do you think would be particularly helpful?

5 Paul and the Ephesian elders[1]

(Acts 20:13–38)

Paul's desire to be in Jerusalem for the Day of Pentecost (v. 16) made it necessary for him to move quickly, and move quickly he did—from Troas to Assos, Mitylene, Chios, Samos and Miletus (vv. 13–15). Knowing that his schedule would not permit him to stop in Ephesus, the apostle sent word to the elders of the church there to meet him in Miletus. The details of that meeting provide us with one of the most powerful and riveting passages in the Bible as Paul says his farewell to these elders.

Curtis Vaughn calls the message Paul delivered to these men 'the most personal and most affectionate address which has come down to us from Paul'.[2] The message falls into three parts:

- Paul's review of his own ministry among them (vv. 18–21). The key phrase in this section is 'you know'.
- Paul's announcement of the sufferings awaiting him (vv. 22–27). The key phrase in this section is 'I know'.
- Paul's charge or exhortation to the elders (vv. 28–35).

The chapter closes with a description of Paul's tearful parting from these men (vv. 36–38).

The atmosphere was charged with emotion. The apostle was on his way to Jerusalem, and the Holy Spirit had testified to him that 'chains and tribulations' awaited him (vv. 22–23).

Paul knew that this would be his last meeting with these elders; they would see his face no more (v. 25). This account provides us with a wonderful basis for considering the theme of shepherding God's flock.

THE SHEPHERD

In verse 28 the apostle says to these elders, 'take heed to yourselves'. He would later, we recall, issue the same exhortation to Timothy: 'Take heed to yourself' (1 Tim. 4:16). The term 'take heed' means, according to J. A. Alexander, giving 'not mere attention but attendance, sedulous and anxious care'.[3] It means we are to develop the attitude that expects danger. It is to pick our way carefully so we can avoid the pitfalls and snares that are all around us.

The first object of the pastor's care must be himself. The shepherd must be aware that the well-being of his flock hinges on his own well-being.

If the shepherd himself is sick or disabled, his flock is in trouble. Who now will feed the flock? Who will defend it? Who will care for its sick? Who will care for the little lambs?

How are we to apply this? If the pastor is physically ill on a particular Sunday there is no problem in finding someone who can step in and fill the pulpit. The point of application is the pastor being spiritually ill week after week and still standing before his flock. How can the flock be properly fed and tended in such a case?

Sadly enough, there are many pastors today who are spiritually ill in one way or another. They may be afflicted with:
- The disease of professionalism, that is, trafficking in unfelt truth

- The disease of infatuation with the world's thinking and doing
- The disease of selfish ambition that causes them to use the flock for their own advancement
- The disease of materialism
- The disease of untamed sexual desire
- The disease of prayerlessness

John R. W. Stott says that shepherds 'cannot care adequately for others if they neglect the care and culture of their own souls'.[4]

Many pastors these days have to say with the Shulamite in the Song of Solomon,

They made me the keeper of the vineyards,
But my own vineyard I have not kept. (S. of S. 1:6b)

THE SHEPHERD'S FLOCK

The apostle also said, 'take heed ... to all the flock, among which the Holy Spirit has made you overseers, to shepherd the church of God which He purchased with His own blood' (v. 28).

What an awesome charge this is! How can pastors ever hope to fulfil it? Taking heed to the flock means ...

TAKING HEED TO THE NATURE OF IT
AND TO THE PRIVILEGE OF SHEPHERDING IT

We should note the Trinity in Paul's words. God the Father is here because the flock is the church of God. God the Son is here because the flock is purchased by his blood. God the Holy Spirit is here because he appoints the shepherds of the flock.

What a privilege it is to be a pastor! He is part of something that involves the triune God! This inevitably leads us to a most important and vital conclusion: the flock does not belong to the pastor. It is God's. Pastors are not, therefore, to be 'lords' over the flock (1 Peter 5:3). They are shepherds of the flock only in a secondary sense. They are undershepherds. Christ is the Shepherd of the flock. Taking heed to the flock also means ...

GIVING SPECIAL CARE TO FEEDING IT
There is, of course, no question about what constitutes the food with which pastors are to feed the sheep. It is the precious Word of God. This Word is sufficient for every member of the flock. It is milk for the very young and it is meat for the mature.

No part of the shepherd's responsibility is more important than continually and systematically feeding his people the Word of God. This means that he is to do doctrinal preaching. There is nothing more shameful and embarrassing than to hear a preacher ridicule and deride doctrine. He only shows that he has absolutely no understanding of doctrine or of the task of the preacher. We remind ourselves that the apostle Paul urged Timothy to take heed not only to himself but also to his doctrine (1 Tim. 4:16). No man can adequately shepherd the flock of God who does not obey this command.

We can do no better at this point than to look at Paul's ministry in Ephesus for a model of the type of ministry pastors are to practise. John Stott describes Paul's ministry in this way: 'He shared all possible truth with all possible people in all possible ways. He taught the whole gospel to the whole city with his whole strength. His pastoral example must have been an unfailing inspiration to the Ephesian pastors.'[5]

Taking heed to the flock also means ...

CONSTANTLY WATCHING OUT FOR
AND GUARDING AGAINST PREDATORS
The apostle said, 'For I know this, that after my departure savage wolves will come in among you, not sparing the flock' (v. 29).

We know something of what took place after Paul's departure. The Judaizers, with whom Paul had had so many confrontations, continued to plague many of the churches for years to come. The Gnostics, against whom Paul had already battled, exerted a powerful influence over many churches. These represent, of course, only two of many heresies.

Some would have us believe that this part of Paul's exhortation to the Ephesian elders is completely without meaning or relevance for us. As far as they are concerned, there are no wolves menacing the flock today. But such people only show a stunning lack of discernment. There are wolves aplenty today. And no shepherd worth his salt can ignore them.

The Judaizer wolf is still with us

The Judaizers taught that salvation was not a matter of a person trusting only in the finished work of the Lord Jesus Christ; one also had to be circumcised according to the law of Moses. The Judaizers, then, sought to mingle works with grace.

How very many there are today who do the same! They turn their faith into a good work by which they earn salvation and add that to the grace of God.

The Gnostic wolf is still with us

The Gnostics claimed to have special knowledge or enlightenment granted by God. How many there are today who ignore the clear teachings of God's Word in order to embrace and advocate certain teachings that God supposedly gave them!

In addition to having to deal with the same wolves with which Paul dealt, we find ourselves facing our own special wolves:

The nice wolf

This wolf has invaded our churches to teach that the only thing one has to do to be saved is to be nice and pleasant.

The life-management wolf

This is the wolf that casts aside the traditional doctrinal understanding of various passages and suggests that these passages were designed to convey truths that help us manage the crises and challenges of life. So the visit of Gabriel to Mary is in Scripture not, as you might suppose, to take us one step further down the road of redemption, but to teach us how to deal with interruptions. The story of David and Goliath is not in Scripture to show us how God raised up a deliverer for his people when true faith had faltered in Israel and, in so doing, to point us to Christ, but rather to show us how to kill the giants in our lives. The stories of Isaac, Rebekah, Esau and Jacob are not in Scripture to show us how God sovereignly carried forth his plan of redemption by setting Jacob over Esau, but rather to give us clues about how to avoid having a dysfunctional family! And, of course, the ministry of Jesus has now become a rich resource for finding leadership principles.

It is time, in the parlance of the world, to call a spade a spade. The reason so many pastors have gone to this type of preaching is because they want to grow their churches and build a name for themselves, and they are convinced that preaching about sin, judgement, repentance and holiness will drive people away.

These wolves are savage because they all deprive people of the thing they need most: the saving truth of God.

THE SHEPHERD'S NECK

There is one more part of Paul's time with the Ephesian elders that we should take home to our hearts. It is there in verse 37: 'Then they all wept freely, and fell on Paul's neck and kissed him.'

There is, I think, a great deal of consolation in this scene. The apostle had declared the truth of God to these men, and now, as they looked upon him for the last time, they realized how much they owed him. Yes, their salvation was of God, but God had used Paul as the instrument of his salvation. Being fully aware of this and being overcome with emotion, these elders lined up and one after the other embraced and kissed Paul as they wept.

Many pastors are deeply discouraged. They are trying to stand for the truth of God in an age that despises truth. And, as they preach, many of their congregation probably wonder why they seem to go out of their way to be such odd numbers. They sit in their pews saying of their pastor, 'Doesn't this poor fellow have enough sense to know that he could gather a larger crowd if he would preach more timely and appealing topics?

Doesn't he know that people today are far too sophisticated for this type of thing? Why does he insist on preaching things that only drive people away?'

I would offer a word of encouragement to all faithful preachers. God's Word can and does save. And while you have your sceptics, I cannot help but believe that God is using you to plant real faith in human hearts.

I see you now, faithful pastor, coming to the end of your journey. I see you coming into the presence of your Lord, and I hear him say, 'Well done, good and faithful servant.'

And now I see behind him a long line of people. And I hear you asking the Lord, 'Who are these?'

And the Lord says, 'I will let them tell you.'

And so they come to you one after the other to embrace you, and yes, before the Lord finally wipes away every tear, to weep on your neck with gratitude and rejoicing that you faithfully declared to them the gospel of Jesus Christ.

And on that day, you will be vindicated and you will be glad that you took heed to yourself and to the flock of God. You will be glad that you stood by the old gospel while others were forsaking it in droves. You will be glad that the sword of the Word cleaved to your hand. You will be glad that you preached the redeeming blood of Jesus Christ.

I urge you, then, my brother, not to give up on the good work to which the Lord has called you. Keep preaching and keep labouring until you hear the Master's 'well done' and you see in eternity the fruit of your faithful ministry.

I urge you so to preach that when you finally die, the most fitting thing to put on your tomb will be the words etched on Spurgeon's:

E'er since by faith I saw the stream,
Thy flowing wounds supply,
Redeeming love has been my theme,
And shall be till I die.

    (William Cowper, 'There Is a Fountain Filled with Blood', 1772)

I urge you so to preach with these words from Charles Simeon ever fixed in your mind: 'let us live for God, and for eternity; let us live as we shall wish we had lived when we shall stand before the judgement-seat of Christ ... Let us go forward in the path of duty, assured that the rest which awaits us will richly repay our labours, and the crown of righteousness our conflicts.'[6]

FOR FURTHER STUDY

1. *Read 1 Corinthians 4:1–2. How does Paul picture the pastor in these verses? What element is essential in order for the pastor to function in the way Paul pictures?*
2. *Read 1 Timothy 3:1–7. What characteristics are necessary in order for a man to serve as a pastor?*

TO THINK ABOUT AND DISCUSS

1. *What do you consider to be the pastor's primary task? Discuss how pastors perform this task. From your own experience, do you consider failure in this task to be rare or widespread?*
2. *What are some of the things you can do to show appreciation for a godly pastor? How can you encourage him to persevere in his work?*
3. *If you are a pastor, how has this chapter challenged you? How has it encouraged you?*

Notes

1. A similar chapter, entitled 'Shepherding God's Flock', appears in **Thomas K. Ascol,** (ed.), *Reclaiming the Gospel and Reforming Churches* (Cape Coral, FL: Founders Press, 2003), pp. 427–435.
2. **Curtis Vaughn,** *Acts* (Bible Study Commentary; Grand Rapids, MI: Zondervan, 1974), p. 124.
3. **J. A. Alexander,** *The Acts of the Apostles* (Edinburgh: Banner of Truth, 1963), p. 249.
4. **John R. W. Stott,** *The Spirit, the Church and the World* (Downers Grove, IL: InterVarsity Press, 1990), p. 326.
5. Ibid., p. 328.
6. Cited by **Gordon J. Keddie,** *You Are My Witnesses* (Darlington: Evangelical Press, 2000), p. 261.

6 Warned and ready

(Acts 21:1–14)

We can call these verses 'Luke's travel log'. The repeated use of the word 'we' tells us that Luke was with Paul on this journey that took them and other disciples from Miletus to Tyre, Ptolemais, Caesarea and Jerusalem. The vivid, colourful details make it apparent that they were supplied by an eyewitness. They also indicate that there was much about this journey that was extremely pleasant. The joy of passing hours and days in the presence of those whose hearts had been touched by Christ permeates this account.

But not everything was pleasant. A dark cloud was brooding on the horizon. This cloud had a name: Jerusalem! Serious trouble awaited the apostle there, and he was twice alerted to it.

TWO WARNINGS (VV. 1–12)

A WARNING AT TYRE (VV. 1–6)
Paul and his travelling companions spent seven days with the followers of the Lord Jesus in the city of Tyre, which was located about a hundred miles north of Jerusalem in the land of Phoenicia.

The disciples there were glad to see Paul, but they were

deeply concerned about his plan to go on to Jerusalem. Their concern was well founded. It was prompted by the Spirit of God (v. 4).

A WARNING AT CAESAREA (VV. 7-12)

After departing from Tyre, Paul and his companions spent a day with believers in Ptolemais (v. 7) before going to Caesarea, where they spent 'many days' (v. 10).

During their time there, they received a visit from Agabus, who was a prophet from Judea, the province in which the city of Jerusalem was located.

Agabus, who had received an earlier mention from Luke in Acts 11:28, came with a disturbing message. He took Paul's belt, bound himself hand and foot with it and said, 'So shall the Jews at Jerusalem bind the man who owns this belt, and deliver him into the hands of the Gentiles' (v. 11).

His message had an immediate and profound effect on Paul's travelling companions and those with whom they were staying: they 'pleaded with him not to go up to Jerusalem' (v. 12).

THE READINESS OF THE APOSTLE (VV. 13-14)

The apostle responded to the pleas of his friends by affirming that he was ready 'not only to be bound, but also to die at Jerusalem for the name of the Lord Jesus' (v. 13).

Willingness to be bound for and even to die for Christ were only two parts of Paul's readiness. As we look into his writings, we find him expressing other kinds of readiness as well:
- He was ready to preach the gospel anywhere (Rom. 1:15).

- He was ready to meet the Lord at any time (2 Tim. 4:6).

The Bible urges all Christians to have a spiritual readiness. We are always to be ready to serve the Lord.

As he does in so many areas, Paul serves as an example here. When it came to the things of the Lord, he was a ready man. How is it with us in this matter of serving the Lord? Do we have anything close to what Paul expressed? Are we ready to do what the Lord wants us to do? Are we ready to suffer and even die for the Lord? Or are there distinct boundaries on our spiritual readiness? Are we more reluctant than ready?

To our shame, some of us must admit that we have a kind of readiness, but it is the wrong kind. It is a readiness to quarrel, to insist on our own way, to criticize and to complain.

We need to rid ourselves of the wrong kind of readiness and embrace the kind manifested by the apostle Paul. How are we to explain his readiness?

Firstly, we can say that Paul was ...

GUIDED BY THE HOLY SPIRIT

This passage presents us with a difficulty. It tells us in two places that people warned Paul about going to Jerusalem, and that they did so 'through the Spirit' (vv. 4, 11). The difficulty arises when we remember that Paul seemed to think that he was being led by the Spirit to go to Jerusalem (20:22–23). How could the same Holy Spirit both be leading and not leading Paul to go to Jerusalem?

The answer lies in distinguishing between what the Spirit was requiring and what he was announcing. In speaking to Paul, the Holy Spirit required him to go to Jerusalem. In speaking to him through the others (vv. 4, 11), the Holy Spirit was announcing to Paul what he was facing in Jerusalem. The same Holy Spirit who required him to go to Jerusalem was preparing him for what he would face there.

Those who think that God is always concerned to make things easy and convenient for his people would do well to consider this passage. God wanted Paul to go to Jerusalem, but he wanted him to know that it would not be easy.

Many preachers these days seem to be dead set on recasting Christianity into some kind of formula for so mastering the challenges of life that all hardships are removed. They appear to have little or no place for the Bible's teaching that God uses difficulties to mature Christians in spiritual things and to conform them more perfectly to the image of Christ.

The main point for us to carry away from this portion of the passage is this: God does lead his people through the guidance of the Holy Spirit. We should also note that the primary way in which the Spirit guides these days is by using the Bible, the Word of God.

We can also explain Paul's spiritual readiness by saying that it was …

MOTIVATED BY LOVE FOR CHRIST
With his eyes wide open to the difficulties ahead, the apostle was still willing to go to Jerusalem. Why? It was 'for the name of the Lord Jesus' (v. 13).

The name of the Lord Jesus represents his person. When Paul said that he was willing to die for the name of the Lord Jesus, he was saying that he was willing to die for the person of the Lord Jesus.

What was there about this person that would create such

commitment? The answer lies in those terms 'Lord' and 'Jesus'.

The person whom Paul was serving was none other than the eternal God himself who had come to this earth as a human being. Why did he do this? There was no doubt or question in Paul's mind. It was to make it possible for sinners to be forgiven of their sins so they could enjoy fellowship with God, both now and for ever (2 Cor. 5:19).

Because Paul regarded himself as being the 'chief' of sinners (1 Tim. 1:15), he could not get over the mercy that God had showered upon him through the redeeming work of the Lord Jesus.

We can only explain the zeal and devotion of Paul in terms of the salvation that he received from Christ. It amazed and thrilled him. Through all the years of his ministry, he was never able to get over the wonder of it all. How sad it is that so many believers today, who owe no less to the Lord than Paul did, seem to have got over salvation! How sad it is that salvation, which is still the most glorious thing any human being can ever experience, does not seem to thrill us as it once did!

That brings us to yet another explanation for the spiritual readiness of Paul. He was ...

FORTIFIED BY FELLOWSHIP WITH OTHER BELIEVERS

Fellowship with other believers plays a prominent role in the verses before us. Consider the following details provided by Luke:

- In Tyre, Paul found disciples and stayed with them seven days (v. 4).

- In Ptolemais, Paul greeted brothers and sisters in Christ and stayed with them one day (v. 7).
- In Caesarea, they were accommodated in the home of Philip the evangelist and stayed with him 'many days' (vv. 8, 10).
- The disciples in Caesarea personally escorted Paul and his party to Jerusalem (v. 16).
- In Jerusalem, Paul was received warmly by brothers and sisters in Christ (v. 17).

Nothing so helps us face the trials of life as having brothers and sisters in Christ near us to pray for help and to encourage us. If we are suffering in these days, let us rejoice in the fellowship of our fellow-believers. If we are not suffering, let us seek to be true brothers and sisters to those who are.

Guided by the Spirit, motivated by love for Christ and fortified by fellowship with other believers! These are the streams that fed into the river of Paul's readiness to serve Christ and to suffer for him. If we would have the same readiness, we must have these same streams. Are we finding the guidance of the Spirit in the Word of God? Are we motivated by love for Christ to the degree that we should be? Are we drawing strength from fellowship with other believers? If these things are lacking, our spiritual readiness will be lacking. If we want to shore up our readiness, let's make sure we pay attention to these things until we are able to sing,

Ready to go, ready to stay,
Ready my place to fill;
Ready for service, lowly or great,
Ready to do His will.   (Author unknown)

FOR FURTHER STUDY

1. Read Matthew 6:10. What does Jesus teach us to pray for in this verse?
2. Read Romans 8:14. What does Paul promise in this verse? Review Acts 16:6–7. What do these verses show us about the matter of the Holy Spirit guiding believers?
3. Read John 8:42; 14:15, 21, 23. What do these verses teach about loving Christ?
4. Read Philippians 1:3–11 and 1 John 1:1–4. What conclusions can we draw from these passages about Christian fellowship?

TO THINK ABOUT AND DISCUSS

1. Try to get hold of the words of William R. Featherston's hymn 'My Jesus, I Love Thee' (you should be able to find this on the Internet). Read and think about the words. Then go to the Internet to learn more about Featherston. How do these words from Featherston challenge you?
2. What is your spiritual readiness like? Have there been times in your life when you knew that the Lord wanted you to do something/go somewhere, but you didn't want to? Did you obey eventually? How did you feel afterwards (whether you did it or not)?
3. How does God lead us by his Spirit through his Word today? Can we just open the Bible randomly and apply the first verse we see to our lives? Why or why not?
4. How does fellowship with others strengthen you? What can you do to strengthen your fellowship with other believers?

7 In Jerusalem

(Acts 21:15–26)

Paul's plan to be in Jerusalem for the Feast of Pentecost (20:16) was realized. Luke tells us that he, Paul and other disciples 'went up to Jerusalem' (vv. 15–16).

From the warnings he had received, Paul knew that he would encounter trouble in Jerusalem. He might even have wondered if some of this trouble would also be directed at his fellow-believers. He was, after all, a controversial figure. He had been preaching the gospel of God's grace far and wide to both Jews and Gentiles, but some of the Jerusalem Christians had the mistaken notion that Paul had been insisting that Jewish believers abandon all their Jewish practices (v. 21).

A WARM RECEPTION (VV. 17–20A)

If Paul entertained any doubts about the kind of reception he would receive in Jerusalem, those doubts soon vanished, as he and those with him were gladly received there (v. 17).

The leaders of the Jerusalem church agreed with Paul, but many of their people did not. These leaders could have distanced themselves from Paul in order to appease the people, but they did not. Instead, they chose to welcome him warmly.

The same warm-heartedness with which Paul and his company were received should be present among Christians today. How often it is absent! And how sad that is! Warm fellowship encourages us in the work of the Lord and gives the message of the gospel credibility in the eyes of unbelievers. We might say that it provides a climate in which evangelism can thrive. But in a church chilled by suspicion and dissension, encouragement freezes and evangelism dies. So let us make a warm-hearted fellowship such a priority that those around us will constantly be compelled to exclaim, 'How these Christians love one another!'

We do not have to look far to find the explanation for the warmth with which the brethren in Jerusalem received Paul and his party. The day after their arrival Paul met with James and the elders and 'told [them] in detail those things which God had done among the Gentiles through his ministry' (v. 19).

How did James and the elders respond? Luke writes, 'And when they heard it, they glorified the Lord' (v. 20). And they were able to add their own report of success, saying to Paul, 'You see, brother, how many myriads of Jews there are who have believed' (v. 20).

It is obvious, then, that the common bond between Paul and James and their respective parties was the gospel of Jesus Christ. The gospel creates fellowship with God (1 John 1:3) and fellowship with one another (1 John 1:7).

The gospel abounds with wondrous things, but we must certainly say that one of its most remarkable features is its ability to override natural and cultural distinctions and make people one.

A WORD OF COUNSEL (VV. 20B–25)

The Jews in Jerusalem had heard something about Paul that was not true. Paul was supposedly telling the Jews in Gentile cities to abandon all their Jewish practices.

But they had heard wrong! The message that Paul delivered everywhere he went was one and the same: no one can be saved in any way except by faith in the Lord Jesus Christ. It was Christ plus nothing. But Paul had never said, as was believed, that the Jews must, therefore, cease to practise certain things that were part of their culture. His message was that they must not trust these things for salvation, but they were still free to practise them as expressions of their devotion to God.

The difference lay in what they needed to do to be saved and what they could do after they were saved. Gordon Keddie writes, 'Paul drew a very clear line between what was to be required of non-Jewish converts to Christ as necessary for salvation, and what was permissible devotional observance for Jewish Christians raised under the Mosaic law.'[1]

Although Paul's position had been misunderstood, James and the elders thought it necessary for Paul to do something to prevent a rift in the fellowship between himself and the Christians in Jerusalem. So James and the elders proposed that Paul demonstrate that he still had respect for Jewish culture. Therefore, they asked him to join with four men who were going through the ritual of the Nazirite vows and also to pay their expenses.

A SPIRIT OF ACCOMMODATION (V. 26)

Paul could have blown up at the proposal of James and the

elders, but he chose to do as they asked. He did so because he did not have the type of spirit that makes a person think that he or she is right on every single issue. He rather had the spirit that is willing to accommodate brothers and sisters in Christ.

We should learn from Paul that we are not to trouble the church needlessly. He was willing to concede to the Jews and to accommodate them. It was this spirit that enabled Paul to write,

> For though I am free from all men, I have made myself a servant to all, that I might win the more; and to the Jews I became as a Jew, that I might win Jews; to those who are under the law, as under the law, that I might win those who are under the law; to those who are without law, as without law (not being without law toward God, but under law toward Christ), that I might win those who are without law; to the weak I became as weak, that I might win the weak. I have become all things to all men, that I might by all means save some. Now this I do for the gospel's sake, that I may be partaker of it with you. (1 Cor. 9:19–23)

Accommodation did not mean compromising the truth of the gospel. No, not for a moment! It was rather a willingness to be accommodating on non-essential matters. Paul would have embraced this slogan: 'In essential things, unity; in non-essential things, liberty; in all things, charity.'[2]

We have in this passage, then, a bird's-eye view of Christian fellowship: warm-hearted, gospel-centred and accommodating! May God help us to understand and to implement these things!

FOR FURTHER STUDY

1. Read Philippians 2:1–7. What things does Paul commend as ways to improve Christian fellowship? Who should be our example in this?
2. Read 1 John 1:3, 7. What does John teach in these verses about Christian fellowship? What light do these verses shed on whether we can have Christian fellowship with those who don't believe the gospel?

TO THINK ABOUT AND DISCUSS

1. Name some things that can hinder Christian fellowship. How can these things be overcome?
2. Think honestly about the depth of fellowship in your church. Are Christians truly one, or are there divisions along the lines of age, wealth or race, for example? How can your church improve in this area? What steps can you personally take to improve your fellowship with other believers?

Notes

1 **Gordon J. Keddie,** *You Are My Witnesses* (Darlington: Evangelical Press, 2000), p. 270.
2 Attributed to St Augustine of Hippo (AD 354–430).

8 Suffering in Jerusalem

(Acts 21:26–36)

While Paul was in the process of complying with the request of James and the elders (v. 26), the predicted storm of adversity burst upon him with fury. It began with 'the Jews from Asia' (v. 27). These men, who had come to Jerusalem for the Feast of Pentecost, fancied that they knew Paul very well. Several of them may have come from Ephesus, where Paul had conducted a settled and sustained ministry.

PAUL FALSELY ACCUSED (VV. 27–29)

The Jews from Asia did not know Paul as well as they thought. Seeing him in the temple in Jerusalem, they began to cry out, 'Men of Israel, help! This is the man who teaches all men everywhere against the people, the law, and this place; and furthermore he also brought Greeks into the temple and has defiled this holy place' (v. 28).

Were these charges accurate? Was Paul really teaching against his people, the law of Moses and the temple? The answer, of course, is that Paul was doing no such thing. He was preaching and teaching the gospel of the Lord Jesus Christ. This did not constitute an assault on the Jews, the law or the temple. The Lord Jesus came to save the Jews, fulfil the law and be everything that the temple anticipated.

Paul's haters heard the apostle's preaching, and the face they put on it was this: it was all designed to overthrow the Jewish religion! It is evident that these men had no regard for the truth. Having seen Trophimus, who was Greek, with Paul in the city, they falsely assumed that Paul had taken him into the temple.

PAUL VICIOUSLY ATTACKED (VV. 30-32)

Falsehood often wins the victory, and it certainly did on this day. Luke says, 'all the city was disturbed' (v. 30). This disturbance resulted in a mob seizing Paul, dragging him out of the temple and shutting its doors (v. 30). In the grip of a strange madness, they saw nothing wrong with killing Paul, which they fully intended to do (v. 31), but at the same time they wanted to safeguard the sacredness of the temple. Killing, which was condemned by the very law for which they were zealous, was OK as long as the temple was not profaned in the process! Do we smell here the stench of hypocrisy?

Fuelled by intense hatred for Paul, the mob was set on beating him to death (v. 32).

PAUL PROVIDENTIALLY ARRESTED (VV. 31-36)

The mob would have succeeded in dispatching Paul from this life had it not been for the commander of the Roman garrison. Hearing about the uproar (v. 31), he immediately sent his soldiers to put a stop to it. The commander took Paul into custody, binding him with two chains (v. 33). Unable to determine the cause of the problem, the commander ordered his men to take Paul away (v. 34).

That did not end the furore. Another attempt by the mob to

seize Paul was aborted by the soldiers carrying him away as the crowd cried, 'Away with him!' (vv. 35–36).

Are we inclined to think that it was a stroke of luck for Paul that the Roman commander intervened when he did? There was no luck to it! God was using that commander to protect his apostle! Alexander Maclaren observes, 'The Caesars were ... yoked to Christ's chariot, though unwitting and unwilling.'[1]

The connecting link between Paul's experience in Jerusalem and our lives is suffering. Paul suffers here.

- His actions are misunderstood and misrepresented (vv. 27–29).
- He is rudely seized and dragged out of the temple (v. 30).
- He is targeted for killing (v. 31) and beaten (v. 32).
- He is bound with chains (v. 33).
- He hears the cry 'Away with him' (v. 36).

When Paul was converted, the Lord Jesus made it clear that he was called to suffering (9:16), and this mob action constituted one fulfilment of that promise.

This passage is of interest to us because we also know about suffering. No, we do not say for a single moment that we have suffered on the same scale as Paul. But we still suffer. The fact that our pain is less than another's does not mean that it is not real.

We always have the tendency to be surprised when suffering comes our way. We should not be. The same God who promised that Paul would suffer has also promised that all his people will suffer (14:22; 2 Tim. 3:12; 1 Peter 4:12). Someone has well said, 'God has had only one Son without sin, but none without suffering.'

So the question before us is this: Why does God regard it as being essential for his people to suffer? Why has God not chosen merely to carry his children to heaven on 'flowery beds of ease'? The Lord has determined that his people will face two kinds of suffering. The first is what we might call general suffering. The second is suffering of a particular kind. So we must ask about these.

WHAT ABOUT SUFFERING IN GENERAL?

The particular kind of suffering that we will next consider is suffering that comes our way because of our connection with Christ. This is the suffering of persecution. So by the term 'general suffering', I am referring to all other kinds of suffering that Christians experience. Sickness, sickness in loved ones, financial setbacks, the betrayal of friends, natural disasters—these are some of the kinds of general suffering Christians are called to endure.

Why does God allow such things? Scripture certainly does not answer every question we can pose about suffering, but it does give us some insights on the subject.

Firstly, we can say that suffering reminds us of the ugly nature of sin. Mark it down: all the suffering in this world is due to sin. If there were no sin in this world, there would be no suffering.

The truth is that our spiritual senses can get so dull that we forget what a horrible thing sin is. Before we realize what has happened, we have made peace with sin ourselves. We are not warring against it as we should. By bringing suffering into our lives, the Lord reminds us that sin is our enemy and we must never stop being soldiers.

FACE2FACE: PAUL

Secondly, we can say that suffering makes us tired of this world and causes us to yearn for the world to come.

We Christians know that this world is not our home. We know that we are pilgrims here. We know that our citizenship is in heaven (Phil. 3:20). But we all have the terrible tendency to get very comfortable in this world and to start acting as if this world is our home. It is for us a travelling place, but we are always inclined to make it a stopping place. Through suffering, the Lord reminds us that this world is a place of sorrow and heartache. He tells us not to allow ourselves to settle in comfort here, but rather to look towards our true home, heaven, where we will never suffer again.

Thirdly, we can conclude that suffering drives us to seek the Lord and to depend on him.

When things are running smoothly for us, we soon become careless about spiritual things. We forget the Lord and his commandments. Astoundingly enough, we can get to the point that we even use God's blessings against him! We use the tranquil times he gives us to excuse ourselves from attending his house and from serving him. Through suffering, the Lord yanks us back and makes us join the psalmist in saying,

Before I was afflicted I went astray,
But now I keep Your word. (Ps. 119:67)

That brings us to raise a second question:

WHAT ABOUT A PARTICULAR KIND OF SUFFERING?
In the passage before us, Paul suffered because he was preaching Christianity. If we think that suffering for the sake

of the gospel is something that only happened centuries ago, we would do well to think again. In the West there is a rising tide of hatred towards Christianity that promises only to get worse. What can we do in the face of such opposition? We can pray for God to give us wisdom, strength and courage. We can determine that we will suffer persecution in such a way as to give unbelievers a favourable impression of Christianity. And we can and must stop voting for political candidates who, because of their allegiance to certain political philosophies, cannot help but be opposed to Christianity.

Why does God allow his people to experience suffering because of this kind of hatred? Through this he shows us again the reality of Satan, who hates the things of Christ with utmost hatred and who, as a master strategist, convinces people that Christianity runs counter to their best interests.

Through this kind of suffering, God also shows us how utterly blind unbelievers are, and, in so doing, reminds us how very vital is our work of preaching the gospel.

We certainly cannot leave the suffering of Paul in the verses of our text without allowing our minds to gravitate towards the Lord Jesus. As we look carefully at our Bibles, we will see that God has included many, many reminders of Christ. Often these reminders pop up in very unlikely places. In this passage we are reading about the sufferings of Paul. He is beaten and bound, and he hears the cry 'Away with him!' As we read these details, we find ourselves thinking that it all sounds so very familiar. Then it hits us! Jesus suffered these things and even more!

And we realize again that Scripture has once again done its work. It has pointed us to Jesus and his redeeming work!

We never advance so far in spiritual things that we do not

need to be reminded of Jesus and his suffering for us. And each time we are reminded of Jesus and his suffering, we realize that whatever we are called to suffer on his behalf is small compared with what he suffered for us. The remembrance of him causes us to have an entirely different view of our suffering. We find ourselves saying these words: 'Will my suffering bring honour to him who suffered for me? Then let me suffer this and a thousand things more! No amount of suffering can ever repay the debt of love I owe to the one who loved me and gave himself for me.'

FOR FURTHER STUDY

1. Read Romans 8:18. What does Paul affirm about suffering in this verse?
2. Read 1 Peter 4:12–19. What does the apostle Peter teach in these verses about the proper way for Christians to respond to suffering? Why can Christians rejoice in their suffering, according to Peter?

TO THINK ABOUT AND DISCUSS

1. Can you think of additional reasons why God allows his people to suffer, other than the ones mentioned in this chapter?
2. Make a list of people in your church who are experiencing 'general suffering' at this time. What can you do to help them?
3. In what ways are Christians in the West suffering because of the gospel? Can you think of people in your church who are, for example, facing difficult situations or opposition at work or among their families, just because they are Christians? How can your church support such people?

Note

1 **Alexander Maclaren,** *Expositions of Holy Scripture*, vol. xii (Grand Rapids, MI: Baker, 1974), p. 257.

9 Addressing the mob

(Acts 21:37–22:29)

As Paul was being carried by the Roman soldiers away from the bloodthirsty mob, he asked the commander's permission to speak to those who passionately desired to take his life. The apostle wanted to answer the question that was hovering in the agitated minds of that angry mob: Why was Paul making such a pest of himself?

The uproar in Jerusalem was due to Paul's going from city to city to tell the Gentiles that they could be saved without becoming Jews. In so doing, he was going against the accepted wisdom of the day. The poll had been taken. The results were in: Gentiles could not be saved apart from becoming Jews! So why couldn't Paul go along with the programme? Why did he insist on making a nuisance of himself?

Those who were opposing Paul were doing so because they were convinced that he was doing what he was doing on his own! They thought that he was this odd fellow who one day got together with some of his friends and said, 'We need to shake things up! Let's say this crucified Jesus was really the Messiah! And let's go tell the Gentiles that they can only be saved by believing in this crucified Jesus!' As far as his Jewish adversaries were concerned, Paul had gone to the Gentiles as a result of his own eccentric ideas.

Paul answered that question by telling those in the mob three things. As we look at his address, we can essentially put three statements in his mouth. First, he said ...

'I WAS JUST LIKE YOU' (22:1–5)
Paul understood the fevered mob. There was a time when he had that same fever. Speaking in the Hebrew language, he pointed out that he was a Jew of the Jews. Brought up in Jerusalem, taught by the revered Gamaliel, schooled to render the strictest obedience to the law—this was Paul. All that background and learning came together to make him very much like the people he was addressing, as he noted in these words: 'I ... was zealous toward God as you all are today' (v. 3).

Had that mob tried to put him to death? Paul understood. He said, 'I persecuted this Way to the death' (v. 4). We recall, of course, that Paul stood by in hearty agreement as the saintly Stephen was stoned (7:54–8:1). Even when he was binding and imprisoning Christians, it was apparently with a view to them being punished by death (vv. 4–5).

It was apparent to the angry mob that while Paul was once like them, he was not so now. He was now promoting the very thing that he had once tried to destroy. What had produced the change? Paul gave them the answer:

'THE RISEN CHRIST STEPPED IN' (22:6–16)
Having received authority from the high priest and 'the council of the elders', Paul had made his journey to Damascus to arrest the Christians he hated so much and bring them back to Jerusalem (v. 5).

He never got to arrest Christians in Damascus because he became one before he got there. As he rode along, he was enveloped by 'a great light from heaven' (v. 6). So brilliant was this light that Paul fell to the ground (v. 7). By the way, this part of Paul's experience was witnessed by others (v. 9).

While he was lying there in the dust of the road, the Lord Jesus himself spoke to Paul: 'Saul, Saul, why are you persecuting Me?' (v. 7).

Upon hearing these words, Paul asked, 'Who are You, Lord?' (v. 8). He must have been astonished beyond measure to hear this answer: 'I am Jesus of Nazareth, whom you are persecuting.'

What was going on? Paul was receiving revelation. Things were being revealed to him by the Lord himself. Quick as a flash, Paul understood things he had not understood before. One was that Jesus had indeed risen from the grave. Another was that his resurrection proved him to be what Christians had been claiming—God in human flesh. Yet another was that the very people he had been persecuting were completely correct to believe in Jesus.

It all hit Paul in an instant and with terrific force, and it changed him for ever. He was so changed that he himself became one of the greatest evidences for Christianity.

Having affirmed that he used to be like the people in the mob, and having affirmed that he had been changed by the living Christ, Paul concluded by saying...

'NOW I AM THE WAY I AM' (22:17–21)

After returning to Jerusalem from Damascus, Paul had gone to the temple to pray. While so engaged, he fell into a trance

(v. 17). Then the Lord spoke to him. His own people, the Jews, would not receive his message about the risen Christ. So he needed to hasten out of Jerusalem and begin preaching the gospel of Christ to the Gentiles (vv. 18–21).

So Paul explained to his angry hearers why he had been preaching to the Gentiles. It was not something he had come up with on his own. It was not on his own initiative. It was not something he did as a result of his own thinking. He took it up because the risen Lord had revealed himself to him, and had also revealed that he was to preach to the Gentiles.

Paul, then, believed as he did and acted as he did because of the truth that had been revealed to him both on the Damascus Road and later.

Many wonder about Christians today just as that mob wondered about Paul so long ago. As far as they are concerned, religion is a very simple matter. You take a poll and find out what the majority of people believe, and that becomes what you believe and teach. If most believe that they are not sinners, Christians have no right to teach that they are! If most believe that all are headed for heaven, Christians have no right to suggest otherwise! If most believe that all religions are equal in value, Christians should not promote their own religion as the truth!

The great question surging through the minds of many is this: Why can't Christians of the evangelical stripe get with the programme? Why can't they accept what everyone else accepts and quit being nuisances?

They make no bones about it—Christians make them uncomfortable! Very uncomfortable! But they are not uncomfortable with all who wear the Christian label. They can tolerate those who are of a more liberal stripe. But conservative Christians bother them. These uncomfortable people have nothing but disdain for Christians who believe these things:

- Men and women are, by nature, sinners and must be saved from their sins.
- Men and women cannot save themselves from their sins by their good works.
- Jesus Christ alone is the way of salvation.
- Those who do not receive Jesus are destined to be separated from God for ever.

The one aspect that the opponents of Christianity never stop to consider is the same aspect that Paul's opponents refused to consider, namely, that Christians believe as they do because of truths that have been revealed by God. No, we do not claim to have experienced anything like what Paul experienced when the Lord Jesus revealed himself to him. But we are no less the products of revelation than Paul was.

The same Lord Jesus who revealed himself to Paul has developed another mode of revelation. It is the Bible.

We do not believe in the sinfulness of human beings merely because we choose to do so, but rather because the Bible affirms this sinfulness. We do not believe in the helplessness of human beings to save themselves because we want to be difficult and overbearing, but because the Bible insists that we believe this. We do not believe Jesus Christ is the only way of salvation just so we can make ourselves unpopular, but rather because this truth is revealed in the Bible. We do not believe in divine judgement because we want to be out of step with modern thinking, but rather because the Bible affirms this to be true.

And what about the Bible? Is it really divine revelation? Is it really truth revealed by God? The apostle Paul, who received direct revelation from Jesus, insists that it is (2 Tim. 3:16–17). Fulfilled prophecies tell us that it is. Its correspondence to what we see in human nature and human affairs affirms that it is. The changed lives of those who have embraced the Bible tell us that it is.

If we have in the Bible revealed truth from God, the proper question is not why Christians believe as they do. It is rather why so many reject the truth that God himself has revealed.

FOR FURTHER STUDY

1. Read Matthew 16:15–17. How did Jesus explain Simon Peter's good answer?
2. Read 1 Corinthians 2:6–16. How do Christians possess 'the wisdom of God'? Why do unbelievers reject this wisdom?
3. Read 2 Corinthians 4:3–6. How does Paul explain unbelievers rejecting the truth of God?

TO THINK ABOUT AND DISCUSS

1. How do you explain the increasing hostility towards biblical Christianity in the West? How do you think Christians should respond to this? What can we learn from Paul's response?
2. How would you respond to someone who doubts that the Bible contains God's revealed truth? How would you explain how you have come to believe the Bible to be true?

10 Standing for Jesus in a non-Jesus setting

(Acts 22:30–23:11)

This passage relates Paul's appearance before the Sanhedrin, a Jewish court. The Roman commander who had rescued Paul from the mob had a problem on his hands. Paul was both a Jew and a citizen of Rome. Before the commander could figure out what to do with him, he had to determine the nature of Paul's offence (22:30).

The Sanhedrin consisted of members of the two major religious sects of the day: Pharisees and Sadducees. While these men were divided on some matters, they were united in their belief that Jesus of Nazareth was not the Messiah of Israel, but was, rather, an imposter. Paul, on the other hand, was a firm believer in the opposite. So we have here a 'Jesus man' standing in a non-Jesus setting.

This is the point of contact between this passage and us. We who know the Lord Jesus are called to live out our faith in a non-Jesus world. Many of the elite on the East and West Coasts of America are known to refer to the middle of the country as 'Jesus land'. But opposition to the Lord Jesus and to his people exists throughout the United States and around the world.

How should Christians conduct themselves in this situation? We can look to Paul's conduct before the Sanhedrin for guidance.

PAUL'S GOOD CONSCIENCE (23:1)
When Paul faced the council, the first words out of his mouth were, 'Men and brethren, I have lived in all good conscience before God until this day.' Paul was not claiming to be perfect. He had not always done the right thing. He knew that very well! But at every stage in his life, he did that which he thought at the moment to be right. Persecuting the church was not right, but when Paul was doing it he thought he was right. We may assume that Paul was about to add that this conscience would not allow him to do the things of which he was accused (21:28). But he was not allowed to continue! Ananias, the high priest, commanded him to be smacked in the mouth! Albert Barnes writes of Ananias and the Sanhedrin, 'Their feelings had been excited to the utmost; they regarded him as certainly guilty; they regarded him as an apostate; and they could not bear it that he, with such coolness and firmness, declared that all his conduct had been under the direction of a good conscience.'[1]

In our own non-Jesus world, we Christians must live conscientiously. We must do those things that we know to be right; that is, we must live according to the Word of God.

What does the Word of God require of us in a world that is opposed to us? It requires that we live in such a way that we do not provoke hostility but rather defuse it (1 Peter 2:11–15). In other words, while we stand for the truth of God, we must make sure that we are opposed because of the truth and not because we are loud-mouthed and obnoxious.

PAUL'S BOLDNESS (23:2-5)

The punch in the mouth was too much for Paul. Here was the high priest, the supposed guardian of the law, issuing an unlawful command! Enraged by this, Paul did not hesitate to point out the hypocrisy (v. 3).

When Paul was rebuked for answering the high priest in such a manner, he seems to have apologized (v. 5). But Paul was not apologizing. He agreed with the teaching of Scripture that one should not speak evil of the ruler of the people, but this Ananias was the high priest in name only. He was so far removed from serving as God intended that he did not qualify to be treated as the high priest. Paul's statement that he did not know that Ananias was the high priest should, then, be taken as sarcasm: could a man such as this actually be considered the high priest?

Gordon Keddie applies this part of Paul's appearance before the Sanhedrin in this way: 'Let the church today speak with holy boldness and call sinners, in high places or low, to account before the bar of God's revealed Word! How will people repent and turn to the Lord, if God's messengers are too timid to speak plainly about the need of their souls and the only Saviour who can save them?'[2]

PAUL'S FOCUS (23:6-10)

Ananias was a farce as a high priest and the Sanhedrin was a farce as a court. Having exposed Ananias's hypocrisy, Paul zeroed in on doing the same with the court.

The members of this court posed as guardians of law and order, but when Paul affirmed his belief in the resurrection, the guardians of order soon gave way to complete disorder (v. 10)! We must not think, however, that Paul invented something on the spot to throw the court into disarray. In mentioning the resurrection, he was giving voice to the central theme of his ministry. He did not forget his focus because he was in difficult circumstances.

It is true that Paul did not specifically mention the resurrection of Jesus. He probably did not have the opportunity! The mere mention of resurrection in general was like a spark in dry tinder!

Gordon Keddie again draws out a penetrating application:

What this ought to say to us today is that we, like Paul, ought to live as the children of our risen Saviour, keeping the focus of our testimony upon the heart of the gospel—the resurrection of the crucified Jesus—and confront the world with our Lord's claims whenever we can. It is to be feared that we too often let the world set the agenda by choosing the subjects upon which to debate and justify their rejection of Christ.[3]

THE LORD'S PRESENCE (23:11)

Paul's mention of the resurrection created such 'a great dissension' (v. 10) that the Roman commander feared that Paul 'might be pulled to pieces'. So he sent his soldiers to take Paul 'by force from among them' (v. 10).

It is a gross understatement to say that Paul had been through harrowing days. In light of this, it is a blessed thing that the Lord 'stood by him' (v. 11) and encouraged him. The encouragement was twofold. The Lord confirmed that Paul had truly testified for him in Jerusalem. He also promised that Paul would 'bear witness' in Rome. The plots against him in Jerusalem would not succeed!

The same Lord who drew near to assure Paul has assured all his people at all times that he is near them as well (Matt. 28:20; Heb. 13:5). We can, therefore, say with the psalmist,

The LORD is on my side;
I will not fear.
What can man do to me? (Ps. 118:6)

What a joy it is to realize, in this non-Jesus world, that God is at our side and on our side!

This non-Jesus world is going to become increasingly so. How should we respond? Like Paul, we must live conscientiously, stand boldly, testify to Jesus and trust the Lord to be near. This non-Jesus world carries an expiration date. It will soon come to a screeching halt, and we 'Jesus people' will finally be escorted into the glory of his presence. There we will be glad that, by the grace of God, we chose to live for Jesus in a non-Jesus world.

FOR FURTHER STUDY

1. Read Hebrews 13:18. How does the author define a good conscience? Read 1 Peter 3:13–16. What does this passage tell us about Christians and their consciences?
2. Read Psalm 27:1–3. How could David be bold in the face of his enemies?

3. Read Psalm 22:11. What does the psalmist say is near? Read Psalms 119:152 and 145:18. What does the psalmist affirm in these verses?

TO THINK ABOUT AND DISCUSS

1. What evidences do you see that we are living in a non-Jesus world?
2. What do you think it means to live with a good conscience? As you think about the rest of the day or week ahead, what will living like this mean for you in practice?
3. Why do you think Christians often seem to fail to be bold for Christ? Can you think of times when you know you should have spoken out boldly for Christ but didn't? What held you back? How can our fears in this area be overcome?
4. How can Christians determine when they should defend themselves and when they should keep silent?

Notes

1 **Albert Barnes,** *Barnes' Notes: Acts, Romans* (Grand Rapids, MI: Baker, 2005), p. 320.
2 **Gordon J. Keddie,** *You Are My Witnesses* (Darlington: Evangelical Press, 2000), p. 285.
3 Ibid., p. 286.

11 Cheering thoughts from chilling circumstances

(Acts 23:11–35)

We certainly have chilling circumstances presented in these verses. Paul has been taken into custody by the Romans to prevent the Jews from killing him. One would think that would have ended the matter, but it didn't. Forty men entered into a conspiracy to kill the apostle.

These men came to the religious leaders with a plan (v. 14). The leaders would ask the Roman commander to bring Paul before them once more so they could more fully inquire into his case (v. 15). While Paul was in transit from the jail to the courtroom, these forty men would attack and kill him. In an act of astonishing irony and hypocrisy, the religious leaders, men who were supposedly devoted to the law of God, agreed with the conspirators.

So Paul's life appears to be hanging by a thread. Chilling circumstances indeed! This is not, however, a passage solely about such circumstances. It is also a passage of cheering thoughts.

What are those thoughts? The first is this:

NO PLACE IS TOO HARD FOR THE LORD TO FIND (V. 11)

Paul was alone in a prison cell. He was hidden from human view. But the Lord knew where he was, appeared to him and spoke to him.

How valuable and precious is the presence of the Lord with his people! The religious leaders were in the temple, surrounded by beauty and splendour. The Roman commander was in the palace, also surrounded by beauty and splendour. But Paul was in a prison cell surrounded by the presence of Jesus Christ. Who was in the best position? Paul! It is better to be in a dungeon with Christ than to be in a palace or temple without him.

When John Bunyan was imprisoned for preaching the gospel, a Quaker minister came to visit him. 'Friend,' the Quaker said, 'the Lord sent me to thee, and I have been seeking thee in half the prisons of England.'

Bunyan replied, 'Nay, verily, that cannot be; for if the Lord had sent thee to me, thou wouldst have come here at once, for he knows I have been here for years.'[1]

Your circumstances may be such that you feel as if God has forgotten you or abandoned you. Listen to John Bunyan! That cannot be! The Lord who loves you and has saved you will never forget you or abandon you. He stands by the words that he spoke to Israel many centuries ago:

Can a woman forget her nursing child,
And not have compassion on the son of her womb?
Surely they may forget,
Yet I will not forget you.

> See, I have inscribed you on the palms of My hands;
> Your walls are continually before Me. (Isa. 49:15–16)

Here is a second cheering thought:

NO THOUGHT IS TOO DEEP FOR THE LORD TO KNOW (VV. 12–16)

Luke tells us that there were more than forty men who 'bound themselves under an oath, saying that they would neither eat nor drink till they had killed Paul' (vv. 12–13). For a while Paul was unaware of this fearful thing. But the Lord was aware of it, and he not only made sure that Paul was aware of it, but also that he got safely out of Jerusalem.

There is great consolation in the knowledge of God. He knows about each and every tear that drops from our eyes. He knows each fear and anxiety. He knows each heartache and heartbreak.

But the knowledge of God is a perfect knowledge. He not only knows these things when they happen; he also knows them before we know them.

But through a coincidence Paul became aware of this plot and made the Roman commander aware of it. That coincidence was his nephew happening to hear of the plot (v. 16).

Coincidence? There are no coincidences in the life of the Christian. There are only providences! Paul's nephew learned of this plot and reported it because God made sure that he learned of it and reported it!

That brings us to yet another cheering thought:

NO PERSON IS TOO SMALL FOR THE LORD TO USE (VV. 16–22)

Here the Lord uses Paul's nephew. We are not given his

name, and we never meet him again on the pages of Scripture. The Lord delights in using small, insignificant people and things and has often done so to the glory of his name. He used Samson and the jawbone of a donkey to defeat the Philistines. He used a shepherd boy and his sling to defeat a giant and bring deliverance to the people of Israel. He used a lad and his lunch to provide food for a multitude.

Many of us think that we are too small to be used by the Lord. The devil is ever eager for us to draw this conclusion. He would have each Christian constantly saying to him- or herself, 'There is nothing I can do!'

But any Christian who is conscious of personal inadequacy can be used of the Lord! The apostle Paul was reflecting on this truth when he wrote, 'For when I am weak, then I am strong' (2 Cor. 12:10).

The final cheering thought that emerges from this passage is this:

NO ONE IS TOO GREAT FOR THE LORD TO DEFEAT (VV. 23–35)

Paul was just one man, and he was the target of forty men! On the face of it, he seemed to have no chance at all. Forty-to-one! The odds were too great!

But look at what happened. The forty never got the opportunity to carry out their plot. The Lord had guaranteed that Paul would go to Rome, and no forty men, four hundred men, or, for that matter, four thousand men could have prevented it. God cannot be defeated, no matter how many plot and connive!

These forty conspirators had placed themselves 'under a

great oath' (v. 14). They would eat nothing until they had killed Paul. They must have got very hungry indeed!

What is there in this passage for us? Let Paul represent the gospel and let the forty men who wanted to kill him represent opposition to the gospel.

Now we have, as it were, a snapshot of our own time. There is so very much opposition to the gospel, and that opposition is so very strong that it may look to us as if the gospel cannot possibly succeed. It may even seem from time to time that both the gospel and the gospel-preaching church are destined to be destroyed.

We must never leap to conclusions on the basis of mere appearances, though. Just as God preserved Paul by defeating the strong conspiracy against him, so God is going to preserve his gospel today. No weapon formed against it will finally succeed!

Let the forces of the devil rage and gather as a flood. God has promised that the gates of hell will not prevail against his gospel-preaching church!

We have covered wonderful ground. Paul was in the midst of chilling circumstances, but the Lord encouraged and protected him. The Lord provided him with cheer in the midst of it all.

The church of the Lord Jesus is facing difficult circumstances today just as Paul did so long ago. Indications are that things will get even more difficult for the church in the future. But we will not be in despair if we will remember these things: no place is too hard for the Lord to find, no thought is too deep for him to know, no one is too small for him to use and no one is too great for him to defeat.

FOR FURTHER STUDY

1. Read Psalm 139:1–16. What does David teach here about the perfect knowledge of God?
2. Read 1 Corinthians 1:26–31. What reason does Paul give for God choosing small and insignificant things?

TO THINK ABOUT AND DISCUSS

1. Try to locate some Scriptures that serve as further examples of the four points in this chapter.
2. Which of these four points is most meaningful to you? Why?
3. Throughout history, many emperors and rulers have tried to destroy Christianity. How many examples can you think of? Think also of accounts in Scripture. Did these attempts succeed? Why not? How should this encourage us today?

Note

1 Quoted in **Charles Spurgeon,** *Metropolitan Tabernacle Pulpit*, vol. lv (Pasadena, TX: Pilgrim, 1979), p. 338.

12 Voices from the cemetery

(Acts 24:1–27)

In these verses, Luke casts a spotlight on three men: Tertullus, Felix and Paul. We are meeting two of these men for the first time. Tertullus appears here in the capacity of a prosecuting attorney. He is here to state the Jews' case against Paul, evidently having been selected because of his reputation as a powerful speaker.

Felix, the Roman governor of Israel, had his headquarters in Caesarea. With Felix, we come to a new emphasis in the book of Acts, that is, the apostle Paul appearing before prominent Roman officials. The God who has used Paul in such mighty ways is now using him in this way.

While these men have been dead for centuries, they speak to us about issues that are just as important today as they were on the long-ago occasion described by Luke in this chapter. The issues of which these dead men speak are spiritual and eternal realities. While many regard such matters as having little or no importance, the truth is that they will matter immensely long after our cell phones and computers have perished! I will go so far as to say that our happiness when we go to the cemetery hinges on whether we listen to these men who are already there!

TERTULLUS: DON'T LET YOUR LOYALTY TO AN INSTITUTION BLIND YOU TO THE TRUTH (VV. 1–9)

While Tertullus was a very bright and gifted man, he was very much 'truth-challenged' on this occasion, falsely accusing Paul of the following:

- Being 'a plague' ('a pestilent fellow' (KJV) or 'a real pest' (NASB), v. 5)
- Creating dissension among the Jews throughout the world (v. 5)
- Being a ringleader of the Nazarenes (that is, a leader of the followers of Jesus the Nazarene) (v. 5)
- Profaning or desecrating the temple, that is, doing something there that was out of keeping with the purpose of the temple and the laws that regulated conduct there (v. 6)

When we scrape away the surface, we have no trouble identifying Tertullus's real message. It was that the Jewish religion, as he knew it, had to be protected at all costs.

What was wrong with this? God had instituted the Jewish religion for the purpose of pointing to the coming of the Messiah. The Messiah had now come in the person of Jesus. The Jewish religion that had anticipated him should now have embraced him, but Judaism had so fallen in love with its anticipatory function that it could not now break with it. It had become so overgrown with tradition that it had completely departed from its original purpose and could no longer see the hand of God at work.

God was moving in the gospel, in Paul and among the Gentiles, but all Tertullus could see was a threat to the institution that he held so dear. So he essentially levelled three charges at Paul: sedition, heresy and sacrilege. This was, of course, a lot of nonsense. Tertullus and the other religious leaders hated Paul because he preached that Jesus of Nazareth was the Messiah.

Although Tertullus has been in his grave for centuries, his descendants still live. All those who are more interested in the machinery of church organization than they are in the message the church was sent to proclaim, the gospel of Jesus Christ, belong to Tertullus's family. There are those who are more Baptist, Methodist, Presbyterian, Lutheran, Pentecostal or Episcopalian than they are Christian. May God help us not to be among them!

PAUL: DON'T LET THE PRESSURE OF THE MOMENT BLIND YOU TO YOUR DUTY (VV. 10–21)

Tertullus has spoken, filling the room, as it were, with great billows of smoke. Now it is Paul's turn.

Paul was under such enormous pressure here that he could very easily have said to himself, 'I had better be careful what I say. I've stirred up enough trouble. I'm already in jeopardy. I had better tone things down.'

But Paul would not allow the pressure of the moment to blind him to his duty to speak for Christ, and his message to us would be to follow his example.

Certain phrases leap off the page as we read Paul's answer to Tertullus:
- 'I confess' (v. 14)
- 'I worship' (v. 14)
- 'I believe' (v. 14—'believing')
- 'I have hope' (v. 15)
- 'I strive' (v. 16)

Paul was in trouble because of his Christianity. The issue standing naked in that courtroom was whether Paul would confess his Christianity. The above phrases give us the answer. Paul was not backing down an inch in his commitment to Jesus.

How he tests us! Are we willing gladly to confess Jesus when the pressure is on us not to confess? Are we willing to say he is the one we worship? Are we willing to say we believe in Jesus? Are we ready to say that the resurrected Jesus is the one who gives us hope? Are we able to say that Jesus is the reason we strive to live conscientiously?

More particularly, Paul had an answer for each charge brought against him by Tertullus:

- Regarding sedition, it was absurd to suppose him guilty, for he had not been in Jerusalem long enough to do this. Furthermore, he had not during that time gathered a crowd or addressed an assembly (v. 11).
- Regarding heresy, he confessed that he was a Christian (v. 14), but he also maintained that Christianity was by no means out of keeping with the Old Testament. It was rather a fulfilment of it.
- Regarding the charge of sacrilege, he insisted that he had not in any way profaned the temple, but had actually come there to bring alms and offerings and to perform the rites of purification.

We come now to the third of the speakers in this chapter—Felix. Here is his message:

FELIX: DON'T LET THE DEVIL BLIND YOU TO THE URGENCY OF THE MOMENT (VV. 22–27)

After hearing the case against Paul and Paul's response, Felix delayed in delivering a verdict (v. 22).

A few days later, Felix had Paul brought in again (v. 24). Once again, the apostle shone brilliantly, reasoning with Felix about 'righteousness, self-control, and the judgment to come' (v. 25). The confessor was still confessing!

Felix responded in these words: 'Go away for now; when I have a convenient time I will call for you' (v. 25).

There is no evidence that Felix ever came to faith in Christ, even though he often 'conversed' with Paul (v. 26).

A well-known story has the devil meeting with some of his demons. The meeting was designed to find a strategy for bringing more people to hell. One demon suggested that they tell people that there is no God. Another suggested that they tell them there is no heaven. A third suggested that they tell them there is no hell. Satan ruled each of these out. Then a fourth demon suggested that they tell them there is no hurry, a suggestion which was accepted.

Felix is calling from his grave to all unbelievers. He is urging them not to let the devil blind them to the urgency of receiving the Lord Jesus. Felix had the opportunity to deliver a correct verdict about the Lord Jesus Christ, but it is very likely that he never did. Now he shouts from his grave to warn us that we must deliver the correct verdict about Jesus while we can.

FOR FURTHER STUDY

1. Read Mark 7:1–11. What were the Pharisees doing out of loyalty

to the institution of Judaism? What was Jesus's response?
2. Read Luke 9:57–62. What did Jesus say about those who delayed in committing themselves to him?
3. Read Matthew 10:17–22. What does Jesus promise his disciples in these verses?

TO THINK ABOUT AND DISCUSS

1. What do you consider to be indications of too much loyalty to an institution? What examples of it can you see in the church today? Think honestly: can you see any traces of it in your own heart?
2. How do you explain Paul's bold witness before prominent Roman officials?
3. Have you heeded Felix's warning? Are you like him, merely interested in Jesus Christ without making any commitment to him, or have you put your trust in him as your Saviour?

13 Casual Festus[1]

(Acts 25:1–27)

Festus, the Roman governor of Judea, was casual when it was not easy to be. His world was churning and boiling with the ferment of revolution and buffeted with the winds of change. Most men were caught up in the fever of deciding the white-hot controversies of the day, but Festus has managed to emerge from the pages of Scripture as one who was content nonchalantly to coast along.

The apostle Paul forced Festus to reveal his casual colours. Paul had been arrested in Jerusalem for stirring up strife. A plot had been hatched by the Jewish leaders to eliminate him before his case could be settled in court (23:12–14). When word of the plot leaked out Paul was whisked away to Caesarea (23:23–24). His case was heard by Festus's predecessor, Felix, but the latter simply left Paul for Festus to deal with (24:27).

Festus heard the charges against Paul and decided to send Paul on to Rome for trial (25:12) when King Agrippa arrived for a visit (v. 13). As something of a diversion, it seems, Festus decided to let Paul appear before Agrippa (vv. 14–27).

The interesting thing in all of this is what Festus said in explaining to Agrippa the charges brought against Paul by the Jews: the Jews 'had some questions against him about their own religion and about a certain Jesus, who had died, whom Paul affirmed to be alive. And because I was uncertain of such questions, I asked whether he was willing to go to Jerusalem and there be judged concerning these matters' (vv. 19–20). How casually these words dropped from Festus's lips! How lightly his tongue tripped over them! As we read them we wish we could reach down through the long corridor of time, lay hands on him, shake him and say, 'Festus, think about what you just said!'

THE SIGNIFICANCE OF THE DEBATE ABOUT JESUS

What was there for Festus to think about? Simply this: the significance of the point of disagreement between Paul and the Jewish leaders. Give Festus credit for stating it accurately. Paul was indeed insisting that a certain man, Jesus, was alive, and the Jewish leaders were insisting that he was dead.

We are used to hearing and reading about famous people who, although reportedly dead, have been sighted. Adolph Hitler, John F. Kennedy, Elvis Presley and many others supposedly concocted very elaborate schemes to hoodwink the public into thinking they were dead, only to surface in a quiet hamlet somewhere.

But the issue between Paul and the Jewish leaders was not whether Jesus had actually died. They were all agreed on that. The issue was whether he was still dead or had risen from the grave.

What made the dispute of Paul and the Jewish leaders so vital? Dead people just do not rise from their graves! And if it can be conclusively demonstrated that a man has risen, we are faced with two massive implications. Firstly, this man is no ordinary man, but is God himself. Secondly, if he is God, he is certainly worthy of our worship and obedience.

If you had been at Festus's side when he uttered his casual words, would you not have been tempted to tug at his sleeve and say, 'Think about it, man! If it is true that Jesus rose from the grave, as Paul alleges, everything is changed, and we cannot go on living as if it had never happened!'

Festus was face-to-face with a claim of monumental significance and he waved it off as though it were nothing. To him it was just a matter of some Jews fussing over their own religion. It never occurred to him that this was not a matter that concerned only the Jews. If a man had indeed risen from the grave, it quite obviously was far more than a matter of the Jews and their religion. If it was only the Jewish population that was affected by death, Festus could have legitimately dismissed the resurrection as something that had significance only for them. But the fact that all those around him were dying, and he himself was facing death, meant that the resurrection of Jesus had implications for all.

A lot of people have more or less the same approach as Festus to any claim of spiritual truth. They think that it applies only to those who have some natural inclination towards religion. They argue that some people are merely religious by nature and it is, therefore, OK for them to busy themselves with such matters. Those who are not so constituted should be left alone. But these people, like Festus, fail to realize that if Jesus rose from the grave, it has implications for them as well, religiously inclined or not.

THE EASE OF INVESTIGATION

It also never occurred to Festus that this was something that could quite easily be investigated and determined. It was not a matter of great complexity that required the work of an expert or genius. Jesus was either dead or alive. This was not an issue that lent itself to ambiguity or neutrality.

When Paul later appeared before Agrippa, he said of the resurrection of Jesus, 'this thing was not done in a corner' (26:26). What did he mean? That anyone who wanted to know whether Jesus was alive could discover the truth easily enough! An event of this magnitude does not take place without creating quite a stir, especially when the dead man appears to various people around the city! And it was no mere handful of people who saw the Lord Jesus after he arose. Paul assured the Christians in Corinth that over five hundred people had seen the risen Lord at one time (1 Cor. 15:6).

And yet Festus lamely confessed to Agrippa that he was 'uncertain' how to investigate this matter (25:20). A trip down to Jerusalem to see the empty tomb and some interviews with those who claimed to have seen the Lord would have gone a long way towards resolving it. Festus's problem was not that he was unaware how to investigate this matter, but rather that he did not care enough to put forth the effort.

With so much at stake one would think that no one would be foolish enough to reject Christianity without first investigating it, but the sad fact is that millions are doing exactly that. They reject it, not because they have conducted a diligent investigation and proven it untrue, but rather because they merely assume it is untrue without having put forth any effort to investigate it at all.

FOR FURTHER STUDY

1. Read John 20:24–29. Who is the resurrection sceptic in these verses? How did Jesus convince him of his resurrection?
2. Read Romans 1:4. What does Paul conclude about Jesus on the basis of his resurrection?
3. Read 1 Corinthians 15:12–19. Why did Paul focus his preaching around the truth of the resurrection? According to Paul, would there be any point to Christianity if Jesus had not risen from the dead?

TO THINK ABOUT AND DISCUSS

1. How would you respond to someone who asked you for evidence that Jesus arose from the grave?
2. How would you respond to someone who asked you to explain why it matters whether Jesus arose from the dead?
3. What are we to make of so-called Christian leaders who deny that Jesus arose from the dead?

Note

1 A similar chapter, entitled 'The Folly of a Casual Attitude about Crucial Truth', appears in my book *How to Live in a Dangerous World* (Darlington: Evangelical Press, 1998), pp. 81–84.

14 On trial for hope

(Acts 26:1–15)

This passage of Scripture contains a surprising phrase. While standing before King Agrippa, the apostle Paul steadfastly maintained that he was on trial for 'hope'. Here are his words: 'And now I stand and am judged for the hope of the promise made by God to our fathers' (v. 6).

We often hear about people being on trial for murder or burglary, but on trial for hope? Have you ever heard of such a thing? You have now!

Let's delve into this matter. We may very well find that it has more to do with us than we might think.

THE POINT OF AGREEMENT

We recall that Paul was standing before King Agrippa because the religious leaders of the Jews had brought serious charges against him (24:1–9). Those charges were first heard by Felix and then by his successor, Festus. Not quite knowing what to make of the case against Paul, and needing to specify charges against him before sending him to Caesar, Festus asked for help from King Agrippa (25:24–27).

It was in his opening words to Agrippa that Paul mentioned being on trial for hope. Now there were several points of disagreement between Paul and the religious leaders of the

Jews, but there was one point upon which there was no disagreement at all. That point was that the people of Israel all shared a hope. What was the nature of that hope? Paul identified it in these words: 'the promise made by God to our fathers' (v. 6).

What was he talking about? What was the promise that God had made to the fathers? It was the promise of the Messiah.

All Jews were agreed that the Messiah was the hope of Israel. He would fulfil the promise that God had made long ago. He would not only come to Israel, but he would also set things right.

THE POINT OF DISAGREEMENT

What a great disagreement it was! Paul had been declaring that the hope of Israel had been fulfilled. He had been insisting that Jesus of Nazareth was the fulfilment. He was the Messiah!

To those religious leaders, this claim was preposterous. It was outrageous! There was so much about Jesus that did not fit their expectations regarding the Messiah. For one thing, Jesus had been brought up in lowly, unimpressive Nazareth. The Messiah would surely not come from Nazareth in Galilee (John 1:46; 7:52)!

Then there was the fact that Jesus had done absolutely nothing to help Israel escape the bondage imposed by the hated Romans. As far as they were concerned, the Messiah would lead Israel to a position of supremacy among the nations. Jesus had not done this! Far from it! Those very Romans had nailed him to a cross. Every Jew knew that being put to death in this way indicated the curse of God (Deut. 21:23; Gal. 3:13).

To the religious leaders this was a no-brainer. For Jesus to be crucified meant that he was accursed of God. For him to be accursed of God meant he could not possibly be the Messiah. Case closed!

THE DECISIVE FACTOR

On the one hand, the Jewish leaders were arguing that Jesus was not the Messiah. On the other hand, Paul was affirming that Jesus was the Messiah. How was Agrippa to know who was right and who was wrong? Jesus could not both be the Messiah and not be the Messiah!

As far as Paul was concerned, there was no reason for Agrippa to be in a quandary about this matter. There was one piece of evidence that indisputably proved that Jesus was the Messiah. It was the decisive consideration.

What was this piece of evidence? Jesus had risen from the dead! This was so massive in its significance that it overrode all the expectations Jesus had seemingly failed to meet.

How did Paul know that Jesus had risen from the dead? He had met him on the Damascus Road!

For a long time, Paul had shared the view of the other religious leaders. He regarded the teaching that Jesus was the Messiah not only to be false but downright harmful. The people who held to it were obviously mad and posed a threat to the well-being of society. They needed to be eliminated at all costs (vv. 9–11)!

We have in Paul's attitude a snapshot of a tremendous shift that has taken place in the West in the past few years. As far as many of the movers and shakers are concerned, evangelical Christians are not just mistaken in their views, they actually pose a threat. They are a cancer that must be removed!

But let's get back to Paul. He was very secure in his belief that Jesus could not possibly be the Messiah. And he was very secure in his belief that he was doing the right thing in persecuting Christians.

If you and I could hurl ourselves back through time, stand beside Paul at this time of his life and ask about the resurrection of Jesus, he would have been quick to dismiss it. He would have said something along these lines: 'There's nothing to it. His disciples stole the body and made up the story of the resurrection!'

Paul's comfortable security was all shattered one day when he was travelling to Damascus to persecute more Christians (v. 12). Along that road, he met the very Jesus whom he so despised! He actually saw him in his risen body—nail prints and all! And he heard him speak. And Paul knew that he had been terribly wrong about Jesus. He knew in a flash that Jesus was risen and his resurrection proved him to be the Messiah (vv. 13–15)!

So now Paul was armed with insurmountable evidence for Jesus. This was evidence that could be taken anywhere. So we have Paul asking Agrippa an unanswerable question: 'Why should it be thought incredible by you that God raises the dead?' (v. 8).

If Agrippa had said, 'I don't think it is incredible', he would have had to explain why he didn't believe it. On the other hand, if he had said, 'I think it is incredible', he would have had to explain why he thought God could not do it.

There is a sense in which every Christian is in the same position as Paul. We are on trial for hope! Because Jesus rose from the dead, we know that we have a glorious future awaiting us. But we find ourselves ridiculed and even hated for holding this hope! This is what makes us Christians, and we are hated for being Christians! What shall we do? Shall we seek political power? Paul gives us the answer. We are to meet the scepticism of this world and its Agrippas by pointing steadily towards that empty tomb outside Jerusalem. That empty tomb proves that Jesus is alive and our hope is well grounded.

FOR FURTHER STUDY

1. Read Romans 8:18–25. What does Paul teach in these verses about the hope of Christians?
2. Read 1 Peter 1:3–5. What does Peter say about hope in these verses?

TO THINK ABOUT AND DISCUSS

1. How would you differentiate the word 'hope' as it is used in the Bible from the way the word is commonly used today?
2. How does the Christian's hope help you in facing the problems and challenges of life? Think of someone you could encourage this week by reminding him or her of the Christian hope.

15 Truths worth repeating

(Acts 26:9–23)

These verses continue Luke's account of Paul testifying before King Agrippa. Paul's appearance before Agrippa was the last of his appearances before prominent officials. Luke recorded these appearances as additional evidence of the gospel breaking through one barrier after another. Acts begins with 120 people shut up in a room in Jerusalem. It ends with its foremost spokesman preaching in unhindered fashion in Rome. All the events between show how it got from such a tiny, unpromising start to such an impressive end.

It is the story of the sovereign Lord. He is the one who caused his gospel to break through barrier after barrier. The gospel of that age is the very same gospel that we believe and preach today. Do we have confidence in its power?

We have noticed that Paul was on trial for hope. He and the religious leaders both agreed that God had promised to send the Messiah. The point of disagreement was over whether the Messiah had come. Paul insisted that Jesus was the fulfilment of God's promise, and the religious leaders were outraged at the suggestion. Both could not be right! Jesus could not both be the Messiah and not be the Messiah!

There can be no doubt that Paul had the better of the argument. The risen Christ had appeared to him on the road to

FACE2FACE: **PAUL**

Damascus! In the presence of the risen Lord, Paul had changed his mind! He had originally shared the belief of the other religious leaders that Jesus was an imposter, but now he knew differently.

In these verses, the apostle describes to Agrippa his conversion experience. This is the third time in the book of Acts that we find Paul's conversion described (see also 9:1–9; 22:3–16).

This is no small, incidental detail. The Holy Spirit wanted Luke to include these three accounts. Repetition indicates emphasis. It is safe to say that the Holy Spirit wanted Paul's conversion detailed these three times so that readers of this book could have certain truths about conversion indelibly etched on their minds.

Vital truths bear repeating, and Paul's conversion presents us with the following vital truths.

CONVERSION TO CHRIST IS A GRACIOUS EXPERIENCE (VV. 9–13)
This means that conversion comes about as a result of God graciously working in the mind and heart of the sinner.

How much credit can we give to Paul for his conversion? He was riding to Damascus to either execute or imprison Christians. Becoming one of them was the farthest thing from his mind, but that is exactly what took place.

Paul was converted not through any effort of his own, but rather through the Lord stepping in and changing him.

Much of his conversion was unique. Converts to Christ do not all get blinded by a heavenly light and thrown to the ground. But all do owe their conversion to the grace of God no less than Paul himself did (Eph. 2:8–9).

For how much of your salvation do you take credit? Do you commend yourself for having the good sense to see the depth and guilt of your sin? Do you congratulate yourself for having the strength of will to reject your sins and turn to Christ? If so, you have not yet grasped the nub of the matter. Salvation is all God's work. The only thing you contribute to it is your sin! All the rest is fully of God. If you have seen your sin, it is because of God's grace. If you have hated your sin, it is because of God's grace. If you have turned from your sin, it is because of God's grace. If you have received the Lord Jesus and his redeeming work, it is because of God's grace. So join the hymn-writer Robert Robinson in exclaiming,

Oh, to grace how great a debtor
Daily I'm constrained to be!
('Come, Thou Fount of Every Blessing', 1758)

CONVERSION IS ALWAYS PERSONAL IN NATURE (V. 14)

After Paul hit the ground, he heard a voice call his name: 'Saul, Saul.'

Saul was being dealt with as an individual. Others were with him (9:7), but he alone was singled out.

There is no group plan when it comes to salvation. We are not saved as families or nations or churches. We are saved as individuals!

Every child of God knows something about this matter of being personally dealt with. It may be that Joe Believer attended church services for months or even years, perhaps to please his wife or to be with friends. As he sat in those services, the Christian message meant nothing at all to him. But then one day, he was surprised—surprised by grace! On that day, it all began to make sense to him, and he found himself intensely interested. He felt as if the message of the pastor was just for him; that it had his name on it. What was happening? The church was the same, the pews were the same, the pastor was the same and the message was the same. But in another sense, nothing was the same, because this man was now being personally dealt with by the Spirit of God.

This awareness of being dealt with in a personal way is always present in real conversion. We may not have the dramatic elements Paul had when he was converted, but we do have this element of personal dealing.

CONVERSION IS AN ENLIGHTENING EXPERIENCE (VV. 15–18)

Paul was so very sure of things as he made his way to Damascus. He was sure that Jesus was not the Messiah, that he had not risen from the dead and that believers in Jesus constituted a real menace.

He was also sure about himself. He thought that, in persecuting those hateful Christians, he was rendering service to God.

Everything changed in a flash! Lying there on the road, Paul had his mind changed about Jesus. If Jesus was there speaking to him, Jesus must be alive! And if he was alive, he must be the Messiah, the Lord and the Saviour!

Paul also had his mind changed about himself. He saw that in fighting the name of Jesus he had not been serving God but opposing him!

He further realized that in opposing God, he had been opposing himself. He had been kicking 'against the goads'

(v. 14). He had been like the stubborn ox who, in kicking the sharp sticks on the front of the oxcart, hurt not the cart but only himself.

This is one of the constant, ongoing features of true conversion to Christ. It always enlightens the mind. Before he was saved, Paul thought that he was in the light. When he was saved, he saw that he had really been in darkness. All believers could add their own word of testimony at this point.

CONVERSION IS A LIFE-CHANGING EXPERIENCE (VV. 19–25)
Paul did not get up from the road, dust himself off and say, 'Now, let's go get those Christians!' Not at all! He rather began to preach the very message that he had sought to destroy.

True conversion always changes lives! How sorely the church needs to recover this truth! Many these days do not expect conversion to make a difference. It is now regarded as not at all unusual for people to be saved and go right on living as they did before. But the testimony of Scripture is clear: being saved means being changed, and not being changed means not being saved.

There are, of course, both usual and unusual elements in the conversion of Paul, and the devil, master-trickster that he is, would have us believe that we must have the unusual elements and not the usual elements. Just the opposite is the case. We need not have the unusual to be saved, but we must have the usual, and the usual consists of being visited by the God of grace in a personal way that enlightens the mind and changes the life.

FOR FURTHER STUDY

1. Read Romans 11:6. Why can salvation not be partly God's work and partly our work? What other Scriptures teach that we contribute nothing to our salvation?
2. Read 2 Corinthians 4:3–4. Why does the unbeliever have to be enlightened to be saved?

TO THINK ABOUT AND DISCUSS

1. What is your definition of grace?
2. Think back to your own conversion. Can you now see the ways in which God was working in your life to bring you to himself?
3. What answer would you give to someone who thinks that he or she has not been converted because he or she did not have a dramatic experience?
4. What would you say to people who call themselves Christians but think that it doesn't matter how they live?

16 Dead men and modern positions

(Acts 26:24–32)

These verses call three men to our attention: Festus, Agrippa and Paul. We are looking at these men, not because we have some sort of unusual fascination with dead men, but rather because they represent positions that are still with us today.

What should we say about Festus? What position does he represent? We can say that he was …

THE TOLERANT MAN WHO WAS INTOLERANT (VV. 24–25)

As he was making his defence before Agrippa, Paul was suddenly interrupted by Festus, who said very loudly, 'Paul, you are beside yourself! Much learning is driving you mad!' (v. 24).

Festus was angry, and he didn't care who knew it! What made him so angry? What triggered his outburst? Paul had appeared before him on a previous occasion (25:6–12), and there was no such outburst then.

The answer lies in Paul's statements about taking the gospel to the Gentiles (26:18, 23).

J. C. Ryle declares that it is a fact of history that many Roman officials 'regarded all religions with secret contempt, as all equally false, or equally true … As for a Jew talking of showing "light to the Gentiles", the very idea was ridiculous!'[1]

When Paul dared suggest that he had been declaring a message that the Gentiles must accept or be eternally condemned, it was too much for Festus! Paul was violating the accepted dogma of the day: pluralism! All religions are equally valid! Anyone who suggests otherwise is crazy! No one has the right to say that he or she is right and others are wrong!

Festus was quite willing to admit that Paul was a learned man. Everything about Paul made that plain. But Paul was a learned madman!

Festus lives every time we pick up a newspaper, turn on the television or surf the Internet. There is nothing that so riles people today as to suggest that Christianity is true while other religions are false. The hostility to this suggestion is so intense that those who make it are considered to have committed a 'hate' crime!

J. C. Ryle writes, '… there are multitudes of people … kind … moral … good natured people, easy to get on with, unless you get on the subject of religion'![2]

The aspect that gets lost in the shuffle is whether there is any evidence to support the uniqueness, the finality, of Christianity. And, of course, there is! That evidence is nothing less than the resurrection of Jesus (v. 23)!

But Festus, priding himself on his religious tolerance, had no tolerance at all for the teaching of Jesus's resurrection.

We come now to Agrippa. What are we to say about him? What position does he represent? We must say that Agrippa was …

THE KNOWLEDGEABLE MAN WHO WAS IGNORANT (VV. 26–28)

Paul didn't spend much time responding to Festus. He rather

turned his attention to Agrippa, who did not share Festus's intolerance. Agrippa knew the facts (vv. 26–27). He knew about Jesus rising from the grave. He knew about Jesus fulfilling the Old Testament prophecies. Would he now go beyond mere head knowledge? Would he commit himself to Christ?

Paul appealed to him to do so, but Agrippa refused.

There is a debate about what Agrippa actually said in response to Paul, but the fact that Paul wished that Agrippa would be 'altogether' like himself (v. 29) gives us a clue. Agrippa was almost there. Paul wanted him to be 'all the way' there!

While the number of Festuses in our society is ever growing, I do not doubt that the number of Agrippas is still greater: people who do not dispute the facts about Christianity but have never committed themselves to Christ!

Why did Agrippa refuse? We must say that he was ignorant of what really matters. He had not thought deeply enough about the swiftness of this life and the certainty of eternity. He had not thought deeply enough about the awesome reality of standing before the Judge of all the earth. He had not thought deeply enough about the awful fact of his sinfulness. He had not asked himself this piercing question: How can a guilty sinner ever hope to stand acceptably in the presence of the holy God?

He had not sufficiently grappled with the fact of Jesus's resurrection. If Jesus arose, he had to be God. If he was God in human flesh, he must have come to this earth to enable sinners to find God. His death on the cross must have been the key element in that matter of enabling.

When Paul dared suggest that he had been declaring a message that the Gentiles must accept or be eternally condemned, it was too much for Festus! Paul was violating the accepted dogma of the day: pluralism! All religions are equally valid! Anyone who suggests otherwise is crazy! No one has the right to say that he or she is right and others are wrong!

Festus was quite willing to admit that Paul was a learned man. Everything about Paul made that plain. But Paul was a learned madman!

Festus lives every time we pick up a newspaper, turn on the television or surf the Internet. There is nothing that so riles people today as to suggest that Christianity is true while other religions are false. The hostility to this suggestion is so intense that those who make it are considered to have committed a 'hate' crime!

J. C. Ryle writes, '… there are multitudes of people … kind … moral … good natured people, easy to get on with, unless you get on the subject of religion'![2]

The aspect that gets lost in the shuffle is whether there is any evidence to support the uniqueness, the finality, of Christianity. And, of course, there is! That evidence is nothing less than the resurrection of Jesus (v. 23)!

But Festus, priding himself on his religious tolerance, had no tolerance at all for the teaching of Jesus's resurrection.

We come now to Agrippa. What are we to say about him? What position does he represent? We must say that Agrippa was …

THE KNOWLEDGEABLE MAN WHO WAS IGNORANT (VV. 26–28)

Paul didn't spend much time responding to Festus. He rather

turned his attention to Agrippa, who did not share Festus's intolerance. Agrippa knew the facts (vv. 26–27). He knew about Jesus rising from the grave. He knew about Jesus fulfilling the Old Testament prophecies. Would he now go beyond mere head knowledge? Would he commit himself to Christ?

Paul appealed to him to do so, but Agrippa refused.

There is a debate about what Agrippa actually said in response to Paul, but the fact that Paul wished that Agrippa would be 'altogether' like himself (v. 29) gives us a clue. Agrippa was almost there. Paul wanted him to be 'all the way' there!

While the number of Festuses in our society is ever growing, I do not doubt that the number of Agrippas is still greater: people who do not dispute the facts about Christianity but have never committed themselves to Christ!

Why did Agrippa refuse? We must say that he was ignorant of what really matters. He had not thought deeply enough about the swiftness of this life and the certainty of eternity. He had not thought deeply enough about the awesome reality of standing before the Judge of all the earth. He had not thought deeply enough about the awful fact of his sinfulness. He had not asked himself this piercing question: How can a guilty sinner ever hope to stand acceptably in the presence of the holy God?

He had not sufficiently grappled with the fact of Jesus's resurrection. If Jesus arose, he had to be God. If he was God in human flesh, he must have come to this earth to enable sinners to find God. His death on the cross must have been the key element in that matter of enabling.

Everything Agrippa needed was right there in the resurrection, but, intelligent man that he was, he was dominated by ignorance on the most important matter.

Multitudes today are following in Agrippa's footprints. They are brilliant in so many areas. They know technology inside out, but they never think about their souls, and they never think about these words from Jesus: 'For what profit is it to a man if he gains the whole world, and loses his own soul? Or what will a man give in exchange for his soul?' (Matt. 16:26). There is a way to prepare to meet God. That way is Jesus. It is always a fool's bargain not to prepare for eternity, and it is always a fool's bargain to reject Christ.

We can close on a good note by considering the position represented by Paul. We can say that he was ...

THE PRISONER WHO WAS TRULY FREE (VV. 29–32)

What irony we have in this passage! Festus and Agrippa were powerful, rich, and surrounded by comfort and pleasures. We might be inclined to think that Paul would have given anything to trade places with them.

But Paul insisted that he wished that these two men could trade places with him in every respect except for his chains. He wished that they could be what he was and have what he had. What was Paul? A firm believer in Jesus Christ! What did he have? Peace, joy and hope!

If we define success in terms of position, power and possessions, we will have to say that Festus and Agrippa were the successful men in this passage. But God defines success in a different way. Success is accepting his plan of salvation, living for his honour and praise, and going to heaven when this life is over. In light of that definition, we have to say that Paul was truly the successful man.

We do not know what became of Festus and Agrippa. We hope that they rethought their rejection of Christ and received him. But we do know what became of Paul. He is even now with Christ, which is, in his own words, 'far better' (Phil. 1:23). His body, long since turned to dust, awaits the coming of the Lord Jesus, when it will be raised to eternal glory.

There is another person in this passage. Yes, Festus, Agrippa and Paul are here, but the Lord Jesus is also here. And the Christ who is present in this passage is always present and ready to receive, pardon and save all who will turn to him in repentance and faith.

FOR FURTHER STUDY

1. Read Esther 3:1–15. Who is the intolerant person in this chapter? What is the reason for his intolerance? What reason does he give the king for adopting his intolerance?
2. Read 2 Timothy 2:26 and Hebrews 2:14–15. What is the bondage described in these verses?

TO THINK ABOUT AND DISCUSS

1. Try to think of some examples of people (whether known to you personally or in wider society) who pride themselves on being very tolerant while expressing intolerance towards Christians. How should Christians respond to this attitude? Why can't Christians be tolerant of all religions?

2. What is the definition of success in this chapter? Why do you agree or disagree with that definition? Think honestly about your life: your values, your priorities and what matters most to you. Which kind of success are you actually aiming for?

Notes

1 **J. C. Ryle,** *The Upper Room* (Edinburgh: Banner of Truth, 1977), pp. 178–179.
2 Ibid., p. 180.

17 Good things in a bad storm

(Acts 27:1–44)

After Paul's final appearance before them, Festus and Agrippa agreed that he had done nothing wrong and should be set free (26:30–32). But Paul, exercising his right as a Roman citizen, had appealed to go before Caesar, so Festus and Agrippa could do nothing except send him to Caesar (see 25:10–12).

Luke, ever the accurate historian, gives very specific details about the first leg of the journey to Rome. Paul and some other prisoners were put in the custody of a centurion named Julius, who commanded the Augustan Regiment (v. 1).

After noting that Aristarchus was also on board, Luke rapidly ticks off the early days of the journey (vv. 2–8), taking care to mention the kindness that Julius showed towards Paul (v. 3).

At Myra, Paul and his companions were transferred to an Alexandrian ship that was sailing to Italy (v. 6). The pace of the journey had been slow. Contrary winds had compelled their first ship to sail 'under the shelter of Cyprus' (v. 5). More of the same caused their second ship to sail 'slowly' for many days and to arrive 'with difficulty' off Cnidus (v. 7). Passing Crete 'with difficulty' they finally arrived at 'a place called Fair Havens, near the city of Lasea' (v. 8).

After laying before us all these details, Luke draws this

ominous conclusion: 'much time had been spent, and sailing was now dangerous because the Fast was already over' (v .9). The Fast to which Luke refers was the Day of Atonement, which was observed in late September or early October. The lateness of the season prompted Paul to offer this sombre advice: 'Men, I perceive that this voyage will end with disaster and much loss, not only of the cargo and ship, but also our lives' (v. 10).

The centurion, being more persuaded by the helmsman and the owner of the ship, and taking into account that the harbour in which they were anchored was not good for wintering, discounted the words of Paul and set sail (vv. 11–12).

The softly blowing south wind that wafted them along at first (v. 13) soon gave way to 'a tempestuous head wind' called 'Euroclydon' (a north-easter; v. 14).

How bad was this storm? Luke writes, 'we were exceedingly tempest-tossed' (v. 18). A bit later he adds, 'no small tempest beat on us' (v. 20). He sums it all up in one cryptic phrase: 'all hope that we would be saved was finally given up' (v. 20).

There can be no doubt that this was an extremely bad storm. But there was also good in this storm, and Luke identifies for us three very good things.

PAUL'S GOOD GOD (VV. 21–26)

Mercilessly driven and battered by the wind, the ship was tossed from wave to wave as if it were a mere toothpick. When Paul had made his appeal to Caesar, he knew his life could very well come to an end at Caesar's hand. Now it appeared as if he would not even get to see Caesar at all. His future was at best very uncertain and cloudy.

The storm in which Paul and Luke found themselves was so ferocious and dreadful that it might have seemed to them that they had been completely abandoned by God. They were not. Paul was able to report to Luke and his other shipmates that God's angel had appeared to him and assured him that he would indeed appear before Caesar. The angel also guaranteed that all those sailing with Paul would survive the voyage (vv. 22–24).

How good it was of God to make his presence known in that critical situation! The Lord had not abandoned his apostle.

God never abandons his people. He is present to sympathize, to support, to sustain and to strengthen, no matter how severe our trials and no matter how far away he seems at the time! The author of Hebrews gloriously writes of the Lord, 'He Himself has said, "I will never leave you nor forsake you"' (Heb. 13:5).

And how very good it was of the Lord to promise Paul that he and those with him would survive the terrible ordeal (v. 24). On the basis of this promise, Paul was able to deliver this cheering word to his companions: 'Therefore take heart, men, for I believe God that it will be just as it was told me' (v. 25).

Our God is a promising God. Just as God had a promise for Paul in that situation, so he has promises for his people in all their trials and difficulties. Puritan Richard Sibbes wrote, 'God supports the souls and spirits of his children with promises, to arm them against temptations on the right hand and on the left.'[1]

Our business in the storms of life is not to argue with God for allowing the storms to come, but rather to latch on to those promises for help and strength.

Another good thing that Luke stresses in his account of this storm is ...

PAUL'S GOOD CONDUCT (VV. 27–38)

It is fascinating to observe Paul's conduct during the days in which he and the others were engulfed in this fierce gale. He did not simply sit in a corner whimpering, 'Woe is me!' He used the storm as an opportunity to minister to others. Instead of 'holing up' in the lower parts of the ship, as Jonah did when his ship was tempest-tossed (Jonah 1:4–6), Paul was out and about.

We have already found the apostle encouraging the others by telling them of the promise of God (v. 25). We also find him urging them to eat, reminding them that not one hair would fall from their heads (vv. 33–34). All this means that Paul had the spirit of his Master, the Lord Jesus Christ. It is that spirit which put the needs of others above concern for personal comfort.

By the way, the best medicine for us when we are despondent over our circumstances is to do something for someone else. Try it!

Former generations of Christians often spoke of their 'testimony'. They would say that Paul's good conduct in the storm gave him a good 'testimony'. We don't seem to hear the term very often these days. The Christian's testimony is the impression for good or ill that he or she leaves on others regarding Christianity.

Let's face it. Unbelievers like to observe believers closely to see if they are practising their faith and to see if that faith is of any value or help to them in the midst of life's crises.

What if Paul had acted differently in this storm? What if he had gone about complaining? What if he had said, 'I have tried to serve God, and this is what I have to show for it'?

Luke does not tell us that some of these sailors and soldiers came to faith in the Lord Jesus as a result of Paul's conduct, but this we can say without any fear of contradiction: these men would have formed a far different conclusion about Paul if he had complained and grumbled.

As for me, I will not be surprised if I ask someone in heaven's glory to tell me how he came to know Christ, and he responds, 'Have you read Acts 27? I was with Paul in the middle of that storm! And God used the way that man conducted himself to show me that I needed his God!'

Let us learn, then, to see every storm as a golden opportunity to demonstrate the difference that Christ has made in our lives.

That brings us to a final good thing emphasized by Luke:

PAUL'S GOOD OUTCOME (VV. 39–44)

How did things turn out for Paul and the others in this storm? God had promised that all would survive. Did that promise come true? Indeed it did! Luke closes his account with these wonderful words: 'And so it was that they all escaped safely to land' (v. 44).

What a beautiful picture those words provide of what awaits the children of God! We live in a storm-tossed world. And we often forget that this world is not our home. We are just passing through. This world is a travelling place, not a stopping place.

And the storms we encounter, no matter how severe they

are, will never succeed in keeping us from our ultimate destination, which is heaven itself. All God's children will make it safely home! They will do so because the God who saved them through the redeeming blood of his Son is committed to bringing them home.

And we, from the wilds of the desert,
Shall flee to the land of the blest;
Life's tears shall be changed to rejoicing,
Its labours and toils into rest:
There we shall find refuge eternal,
From sin, from affliction, from pain,
And in the sweet love of the Saviour,
A joy without end shall attain.   (David Charles)

    We may rest assured that even though all Paul's shipmates came safely to land, they did not all come the same way. Those who refused to believe the promise of God came safely to land after frantic hours of agitation and stress. On the other hand, those who rested in the promise of God came safely to land after hours of the peace that came from knowing that God would not fail.

    We are living in stormy, stress-filled times, but we don't have to be filled with stress. Even though there are storms aplenty all around us, we don't have to have storms within us. We can rest on the promises of God and be at peace. Ultimately, all Christians are going to land safely on God's eternal shore. The only question is what the journey will be like. For those Christians who make a habit of resting on God's promises, the journey will be peaceful and sweet. For those who have difficulty believing those promises, the journey will be stressful. May God himself help each of us to go to heaven leaning on his precious promises.

FOR FURTHER STUDY

1. Read Joshua 21:45 and 1 Kings 8:56. What do these verses affirm about the promises of God?
2. Read Philippians 2:1–11. What kind of spirit does Paul ask the Philippians to embrace? Whom does he cite as an example?

TO THINK ABOUT AND DISCUSS

1. What stormy times have you experienced in your life? Did truths from God's Word help you to have peace in the midst of the storm? Which of God's promises do you find to be most comforting and encouraging?
2. What practical steps can you take to help yourself cope with the storms of life?
3. Have you witnessed or read about Christians going through stormy times and 'giving a good testimony'? Did their testimony make an impact on others?
4. Think of a person you know (whether a Christian or a non-Christian) who is going through stormy times. What can you do to help that person focus on or trust in the promises of God?

Note

1 **Richard Sibbes,** The Works of Richard Sibbes, vol. iii (Edinburgh: Banner of Truth, 1981), p. 384.

18 A wonderful shipwreck and a glorious snakebite

(Acts 28:1–10)

After their ship was demolished, Paul and his shipmates made it safely to land on the island of Malta. No sooner had he arrived there than he was bitten by a poisonous snake!

Some would say that Paul was certainly having a bad day, and they would give us principles or keys to help us avoid such times. One can easily get the impression that God's major concern is to keep us from having bad days.

Those who have this notion would be shocked to hear someone say that it was God himself who ordered Paul's circumstances. The apostle's bad day came from God!

Many are astonished at such teaching. They start with the assumption that God is love, and they define 'love' to mean that he could never do anything that would cause discomfort to the ones he loves.

The sharp irony is that we ourselves often do things that bring discomfort to those we love. We take a loved one to the doctor, and that visit may lead even to the very unpleasant reality of surgery. If someone were to tell us that taking our loved one to the doctor proves we do not love that person, we would say, 'It proves quite the opposite. I took him to the doctor because I do love him. Yes, it is unpleasant, but it is also for his own good.'

We all understand this in our dealings with others, but we do not always understand it in the realm of God's dealings with us.

What did God have in mind when he put Paul through such a bad day? This account enables us to identify four truths that God put on display through Paul's difficulties. God is still in the business of driving these truths home to the hearts of his people, and he often uses hardships to do so. We do well in the midst of our trials to reflect deeply on these things.

The first truth displayed by Paul's bad day is this:

GOD'S PROMISES ARE VERY SURE
A shipwreck seems to us to be an awful thing, but in Paul's case it was a wonderful thing. God used it to demonstrate his faithfulness to his promise. He had promised that all on board the ship would survive, and they did (27:23–25, 34, 44).

How many times in that chaotic voyage did it appear that God's promise could not possibly come true? But it did come true!

The same God who promised survival for those on board the ship has promised certain things regarding all Christians. One is that the Lord Jesus himself will some day return and raise the bodies of all his people from their graves. That promise may seem to be far-fetched and unlikely to be fulfilled, but God never fails to keep a promise!

That brings us to a second truth exhibited by Paul's shipwreck and snakebite:

GOD'S PURPOSES ARE VERY LARGE

A lot of people are disappointed with God because they believe his primary concern is to make life comfortable and easy. When their circumstances are otherwise, they conclude that God has failed.

Meanwhile, God has said very clearly that his primary concerns are saving sinners, maturing his people and glorifying his Son in the process.

With this in mind, we must say that Paul's shipwreck and snakebite make perfect sense. Why did Paul have to suffer the shipwreck? To get him to Malta so that those people could hear the gospel! Why did Paul have to suffer the snakebite? To gain him a hearing from the people of Malta!

The God who has these large purposes expects his people to so embrace these purposes that they are willing to suffer difficult circumstances! The apostle Paul again serves as a wonderful example in this matter. As we read his letter to the believers in Philippi, we find that he was in prison. But instead of chafing under this hardship, he gladly embraced it and rejoiced that God was using it to advance the gospel (Phil. 1:12–18). If Paul had been concerned only about his own comfort, he could not have embraced God's purpose in his imprisonment. But what mattered most to Paul was the Lord Jesus Christ (Phil. 1:21). So if his imprisonment could promote the cause of Christ, Paul was happy to be in prison.

We come now to a third truth driven home by Paul's difficult circumstances:

GOD'S HEART IS VERY KIND

We see this truth as we think about those to whom Paul ministered in Acts 27–28.

During the storm, Paul ministered to his shipmates. Among these were hard-bitten sailors and tough Roman soldiers. After the shipwreck, Paul ministered to the barbarians on the island of Malta.

How did Paul come to minister to these people? God put Paul in the circumstances that allowed him to minister to them. Why did God put Paul in such circumstances? It was certainly not, as we have noted, to make Paul comfortable. It was rather because the heart of God mercifully yearns for the salvation of sinners.

God used Paul's difficulties to put Paul in situations in which he could preach the gospel to sinners. How very kind is the heart of God! It is so very kind that he even desired these sailors, soldiers and barbarians to come within the sphere of the gospel!

Finally, we must conclude that God used Paul's shipwreck and snakebite to make this truth very plain:

GOD'S POWER IS VERY GREAT

Behind all the events of chapters 27–28 is the invisible hand of the almighty God. Think about these things:
- The ship 'just happened' to hit a reef (27:41).
- The centurion 'just happened' to be near enough to save Paul when the decision was made to kill him and the other prisoners (27:42–43).
- There 'just happened' to be enough boards and pieces of the ship in the right places for all 276 people to get safely to shore (27:44).
- The viper 'just happened' to be in the right place at the right time to bite Paul. Out of the 276 people that landed on the shore of Malta, only Paul was bitten.

- The father of Publius 'just happened' to get sick while Paul was there (28:8).

And the God who caused all these 'coincidences' is the same God who kept the viper bite from killing Paul and gave him the ability to heal the father of Publius and others! This is a powerful God!

By the way, this is what the miracles of the Bible were about. They were not primarily designed to make life easier for people and to get us to desire miracles so our lives can be easier as well. They were rather designed to rivet our attention on the gracious and powerful nature of God.

The same truths God put on display through Paul's shipwreck and snakebite are also displayed in the gospel of Christ. The gospel shows that God is true to his Word, that his purposes are very large, that his heart is very kind and that his hand is very powerful.

And this gospel does its good work for all who truly receive it.

FOR FURTHER STUDY

1. Read Genesis 50:20. How did Joseph explain the difficulties that had come his way?
2. Read Romans 8:28. What does Paul affirm here?

TO THINK ABOUT AND DISCUSS

1. Think of a particularly difficult and trying time in your life. In what ways did God work to bring good out of that situation? Did you learn any lessons about God during that time?
2. How do the four points of this chapter help you or encourage you in particular situations you are facing at the moment?

19 A chained man with an unchained message

(Acts 28:11–31)

After a long and harrowing journey, Paul arrived in Rome. There he was placed under house arrest for two years (v. 30). During this time, he waited to appear before Caesar. We must assume that this appearance took place because of the Lord's promise (27:24). We cannot, however, say what resulted from it. Some think that Paul was released from this imprisonment and fulfilled his desire to preach the gospel in Spain (Rom. 15:28). Others think that his Roman imprisonment ended with him being executed.

While much of Paul's last years are shrouded in mystery, one thing stands out very boldly, namely, Paul's passion for the gospel. That passion remained undiminished and constant even while he was a prisoner. In this passage, we find Paul presenting the gospel first to Jewish leaders who came to him (v. 17) and then to 'all who came to him' (v. 30).

There was something very noisy going on in the world at that time. The Roman Empire, with all its pomp and power, was making quite a racket. There was also something very quiet going on. Paul was preaching the gospel.

Many would conclude that what Paul was doing in his

house was of much less importance than what the Roman Emperor Nero was doing. But the testimony of history is clear. The preaching, teaching and writing of the apostle Paul changed the world. His name is on the lips of multitudes of preachers and teachers every Lord's Day. When was the last time you heard someone mention the name of Nero?

What shall we say, then, about this gospel that Paul preached? Firstly, we must always remember that ...

THE GOSPEL IS ABOUT JESUS CHRIST
When the 'leaders of the Jews' came to him at his invitation (v. 17), Paul persuaded them 'concerning Jesus from both the Law of Moses and the Prophets' (v. 23).

There is no gospel without Jesus!

The word 'gospel' means 'good news'. Why is the message of Jesus good news? It is good news because of the bad news! The bad news pertains to us. The Bible tells us that we all come into this world as sinners. What is so bad about being a sinner? We eventually have to leave this world to stand before God, and God is not a sinner! He, the Judge of all the earth, is perfectly holy. He is opposed to sin and cannot dwell with it.

So the bad news in a nutshell is this: if our sins are not forgiven, we cannot stand acceptably in the presence of God when this life is over. We will rather be driven from his presence into eternal destruction (2 Thes. 1:9).

When we understand this bad news, the good news becomes incredibly good. It is that God himself has done everything necessary for our sins to be removed so we can stand in his presence. What he did, of course, was to send Jesus. Jesus came to this world for the express purpose of taking sin out of the way from between God and us so that we can be accepted by God.

There was only one way for sin to be taken out of the way. Its penalty had to be paid. So when I say Jesus came to take sin out of the way, I am saying that he came to pay the penalty of sin. What is that penalty? It is eternal separation from God. Jesus came to pay that penalty for sinners. He did so on the cross. There he endured an eternity's worth of separation from God so that all who repent of their sins and take him as their Saviour never have to receive that penalty themselves.

That is good news!

Secondly, we must always remember that ...

THE GOSPEL CONCERNS THE KINGDOM OF GOD

When the Jewish leaders in Rome came to visit Paul, he 'explained and solemnly testified of the kingdom of God' (v. 23).

The kingdom of God refers, of course, to the rule of God. This rule is not in a political or military sense. It is not a matter of God setting up an earthly kingdom. It is rather a matter of God ruling in human hearts. God's kingdom is a spiritual kingdom.

How does God set up his kingdom in human hearts? The answer once again is Jesus. By his redeeming work on the cross, Jesus deposes the tyrant of sin that has usurped the throne in the human heart. With that tyrant deposed, God takes his rightful place.

That leads us to a third aspect of the gospel that we must never forget:

THE SPREADING OF THE GOSPEL REQUIRES DILIGENT EFFORT

Paul gave himself unstintingly to declaring the gospel. Luke tells us that he spoke to the Jewish leaders 'from morning till evening' (v. 23).

Luke also conveys the diligence of Paul's preaching by using these words: 'explained' (v. 23), 'testified' (v. 23), 'persuading' (v. 23), 'preaching' (v. 31) and 'teaching' (v. 31).

It should be clear to us that the gospel requires careful and painstaking study. Only then can we explain, testify, persuade, preach and teach as Paul did.

What tragedy it is that so many in pulpits today have absolutely no understanding of the very gospel they are charged to preach, and no willingness to study it!

Finally, we must always remember this:

THE GOSPEL WILL NOT ALWAYS MEET WITH SUCCESS

Paul's preaching to the Jewish leaders caused them to be divided. Luke says that 'some were persuaded' and 'some disbelieved' (v. 24). He adds that these leaders 'did not agree among themselves' (v. 25). Paul responded to their disagreement by pointing out that it was a fulfilment of the prophecy of Isaiah (vv. 25–30). The rejection of the gospel by the vast majority of the Jews opened the door for the Gentiles to hear it (v. 28). This caused the Jewish leaders to have 'a great dispute among themselves' (v. 29).

The gospel has always divided people, and it always will. It will always be opposed. But God's people are to be faithful in their proclamation of it, no matter how much opposition they encounter. Why? One reason is that the gospel is true, and no amount of opposition can change that. Another reason is that there will always be some who will receive it and be saved. Alexander Maclaren writes, 'Let us have confidence in the greatness of the word, though the world may be deaf to its music and blind to its power, and let us never fear to ally ourselves with a cause which we know to be God's, however it may be unpopular and made light of by the "leaders of opinion".'[1]

It is our responsibility to make sure that we have absorbed the lessons of this chapter. We will demonstrate that we have done so if we make sure that we understand the gospel of Christ, that we do not underestimate its power, that we work at spreading the gospel and that we don't allow ourselves to get discouraged when the gospel is rejected.

Paul went on preaching the gospel while he was in Rome. He preached to 'all who came to him' (v. 30), with 'no one forbidding him' (v. 31). What a marvel! The very man who once tried to stamp Christianity out in the narrow confines of Palestine was now preaching it in the major city of the day! We don't have to labour to explain such a thing. Paul has explained it for us in these words: 'the grace of our Lord was exceedingly abundant' (1 Tim. 1:14).

It was the grace of God that saved Paul. It was the grace of God that placed him in the ministry. It was the grace of God that sustained and strengthened him through all his trials. It was the grace of God that enabled him to preach in all kinds of challenging and intimidating situations. Our study of his life should cause us to magnify that grace, to share it with others and to depend on it as we face our own challenging and difficult days.

Let us never forget that the message Paul proclaimed, the

message of Jesus Christ, is the gospel of God's saving grace through Christ. Let us believe, as Paul did, in the power of that message (Rom. 1:16) and let us, again as he did, declare it all around.

FOR FURTHER STUDY

1. Read Romans 1:16–17. How does Paul describe the gospel? Why does he describe it in this way?
2. Read Philippians 1:12–18. What does Paul say in these verses about how God was using his imprisonment?

TO THINK ABOUT AND DISCUSS

1. What conclusions do you draw from God using a chained man to spread the gospel?
2. How would you respond to those who say, 'If the gospel is so powerful, why do we not see more changed lives?'
3. What has challenged you most in this study of Paul's life?

Note

1 **Alexander Maclaren,** *Expositions of Holy Scripture*, vol. xii (Grand Rapids, MI: Baker, 1974), p. 385.

About Day One:

Day One's threefold commitment:

- TO BE FAITHFUL TO THE BIBLE, GOD'S INERRANT, INFALLIBLE WORD;

- TO BE RELEVANT TO OUR MODERN GENERATION;

- TO BE EXCELLENT IN OUR PUBLICATION STANDARDS.

I continue to be thankful for the publications of Day One. They are biblical; they have sound theology; and they are relative to the issues at hand. The material is condensed and manageable while, at the same time, being complete—a challenging balance to find. We are happy in our ministry to make use of these excellent publications.

JOHN MACARTHUR, PASTOR-TEACHER, GRACE COMMUNITY CHURCH, CALIFORNIA

It is a great encouragement to see Day One making such excellent progress. Their publications are always biblical, accessible and attractively produced, with no compromise on quality. Long may their progress continue and increase!

JOHN BLANCHARD, AUTHOR, EVANGELIST AND APOLOGIST

Visit our web site for more information and to request a free catalogue of our books.
www.dayone.co.uk
www.dayonebookstore.com

Face2face series

Title	Author	ISBN
Face2face Daniel	Ellsworth, Roger	978–1–84625–223–5
Face2face David Volume 1	Bentley, Michael	978–1–84625–040–8
Face2face David Volume 2	Bentley, Michael	978–1–84625–015–6
Face2face Elijah	Robinson, Simon J	978–1–84625–011–8
Face2face Elisha	Winter, Jim	978–1–84625–113–9
Face2face Ezra	Hughes, Chris	978–1–84625–298–3
Face2face Joseph	Ellsworth, Roger	978–1–84625–293–8
Face2face Judas	Wheeler, Andrew	978–1–84625–192–4
Face2face Paul Volume 1	Ellsworth, Roger	978–1–84625–294–5
Face2face Paul Volume 2 (Forthcoming)	Ellsworth, Roger	978–1–84625–295–2
Face2face Rahab	Hughes, Chris	978–1–84625–135–1
Face2face Samuel	Ellsworth, Roger	978–1–84625–039–2
Face2face Sennacherib	Anderson, Clive	978–1–84625–076–7
Face2face Simon Peter	Ellsworth, Roger	978–1–84625–092–7
Face2face Tamar, Bathsheba and Tamar	Jones, Julia	978–1–84625–141–2

Face2face Rahab— Encountering the woman snatched from destruction

CHRIS HUGHES

80PP, PAPERBACK

ISBN 978-1-84625-135-1

Can the short account of a brief incident from the life of a woman of dubious character say anything to us today—a woman who lived over 3,000 years ago and whose city was doomed to destruction? Yes indeed!

Here is a very readable devotional book with encouraging insights into a lesser-known but surprisingly significant Bible character—Rahab. Throughout the story of this Jericho call-girl, the amazing grace and purpose of God is seen in both the Old and New Testaments.
—DAVID ABERNETHIE, PREVIOUSLY A PASTOR IN BRISTOL AND EAST CHEAM AND ON THE STAFF OF THE EVANGELICAL ALLIANCE

In less than a dozen short, punchy chapters, we are introduced to the mini-drama of the heroine Rahab in her ruin and redemption, set against the backcloth of 'the greatest story ever told' of the Joshua/Jesus the hero of it all. An excellent resource.
—DR STEVE BRADY, PRINCIPAL, MOORLANDS COLLEGE, ENGLAND

FACE2FACE: **PAUL**

Face to face David volume 1—Encountering the man after God's heart

MICHAEL BENTLEY

96PP, PAPERBACK

ISBN 978-1-84625-040-8

Raised in obscurity, young David would not have featured on a list of candidates for the future king of Israel—but God had different ideas! Read, here, about how God's magnificent plan unfolded in the life of this remarkable man and in the lives of those around him.

Michael Bentley worked as a bookshop manager and served in the British army before his call to the ministry. He has a diverse background, which includes broadcasting, teaching Religious Education, and holding pastorates in Surrey, South East London, and Berkshire, while being closely involved with his local community. Now retired, he lives in Bracknell with his wife, Jenny, and has five children and six grandchildren. He is the author of ten books.

Michael Bentley has an enviable knowledge of the Bible and an admirably simple way of relating its events, and then interweaving the stories with their relevance to our life. Thus, we see how the actions related in the Bible can still be appropriate today in the way we live our lives.

FRAN GODFREY, BBC RADIO 2 NEWSREADER/ANNOUNCER

FACE2FACE: **PAUL**

Face to face David volume 2—Encountering the king who reigned in power

MICHAEL BENTLEY

144PP, PAPERBACK

ISBN 978-1-84625-015-6

Raised in obscurity, shooting to prominence in the nation of Israel, David became a powerful figure and everyone loved him—well, not quite everyone. Read about his battles, his triumphs, and also his troubles in this engaging, easy-to-use guide.

Michael Bentley worked as a bookshop manager and served in the British army before his call to the ministry. He has a diverse background, which includes broadcasting, teaching Religious Education, and holding pastorates in Surrey, South East London, and Berkshire, while being closely involved with his local community. Now retired, he lives in Bracknell with his wife, Jenny, and has five children and six grandchildren. He is the author of ten books.

'Michael Bentley treats the life of David in a simple, straightforward fashion, never losing sight throughout of the practical significance he has for us, and constantly holding before us David's greater Son, the Lord Jesus. A very good and satisfying book!'
ROGER ELLSWORTH, PASTOR OF PARKVIEW BAPTIST CHURCH, JACKSON, TN, USA, AND BIBLE COMMENTATOR

'... a book which is full of wisdom ...'
CHRIS PORTER, EASTHAMPSTEAD BAPTIST CHURCH, ENGLAND

Face to face Elijah—Encountering Elijah the fiery prophet

SIMON J ROBINSON

80PP, PAPERBACK

ISBN 978-1-84625-011-8

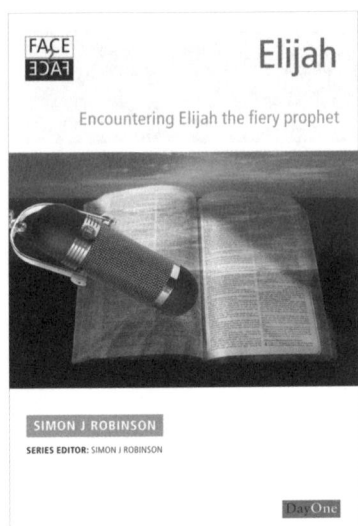

Elijah, the fiery prophet, lived in a time of intense spiritual darkness. People were openly disobeying God's commands, and true worship seemed to have been all but snuffed out. And yet God was still at work! Bringing the power of his Word and Spirit into this situation, he used Elijah to break the darkness and to draw people back to himself. This fascinating encounter with Elijah draws out his significance in God's plan and provides us with practical help to live for Christ in the spiritual darkness of the twenty-first century. Each chapter includes questions and points for reflection, making this an ideal book to be used in small groups or for personal study and devotion.

Simon Robinson is the senior minister of Walton Evangelical Church, Chesterfield, England. He has also written several other books, all published by Day One, including *Jesus, The Life-Changer, Improving Your Quiet Time, Opening Up 1 Timothy,* and *God, the Bible and Terrorism*. He also preaches and teaches in Asia and the United States. He and his wife, Hazel, have two sons and one grandson.

Face2face Samuel—Encountering the king-maker

ROGER ELLSWORTH

128PP, PAPERBACK

ISBN 978-1-84625-039-2

Welcome to the world of dirt roads and oxcarts, cattle and sheep, sandals and robes! Welcome to the world of Samuel—one of the most important men in the history of the nation of Israel. Samuel was a great prophet occupying a unique position in the history of his nation. For a long time, Israel had been ruled by 'judges', but Samuel ushered them into a new era in which they were governed by kings. However, we are not taking this 'face2face' look at Samuel because we are interested in his historical uniqueness but rather because he can help us to know the God who made us and who has a wonderful purpose for all who live for him.

Roger Ellsworth has served as pastor of Immanuel Baptist Church, Benton, Illinois, for eighteen years. He is the author of twenty-seven books, including *Opening up Philippians* and *Opening up Psalms*.

'Roger Ellsworth's book is an extremely relevant and helpful study in the life of Samuel, a much-neglected Old Testament character. It is an extremely practical, pastoral and, most important of all, Christ-exalting-character study at its best and an invaluable addition to a promising series.'

DEREK PRIME

FACE**2**FACE: **PAUL**